50 Premium German Bread Recipes for Home

By: Kelly Johnson

Table of Contents

- Pumpernickel
- Rye Sourdough
- Weißbrot (White Bread)
- Kastenbrot (Loaf Bread)
- Dinkelbrot (Spelt Bread)
- Sonnenblumenbrot (Sunflower Seed Bread)
- Bauernbrot (Farmer's Bread)
- Roggenmischbrot (Rye and Wheat Bread)
- Zwiebelbrot (Onion Bread)
- Körnerbrot (Seed Bread)
- Bierbrot (Beer Bread)
- Laugenbrötchen (Pretzel Rolls)
- Rosinenbrot (Raisin Bread)
- Käsebrot (Cheese Bread)
- Kürbiskernbrot (Pumpkin Seed Bread)
- Sauerteigbrot (Sourdough Bread)
- Vollkornbrot (Whole Grain Bread)
- Dreikornbrot (Three-Grain Bread)
- Helles Bauernbrot (Light Farmer's Bread)
- Dinkel-Sauerteigbrot (Spelt Sourdough Bread)
- Roggenvollkornbrot (Rye Whole Grain Bread)
- Pizzabrot (Pizza Bread)
- Roggen-Kartoffelbrot (Rye Potato Bread)
- Kornspitz (Grain Spitz)
- Kümmelbrot (Caraway Bread)
- Franzbrötchen (Cinnamon Croissants)
- Brot mit Walnüssen (Walnut Bread)
- Knoblauchbrot (Garlic Bread)
- Kaisersemmel (Kaiser Rolls)
- Focaccia mit Kräutern (Herb Focaccia)
- Rosenbrot (Rose Bread)
- Spelt Rye Bread

- Karamell-Brot (Caramel Bread)
- Mischbrot mit Kräutern (Herb Mixed Bread)
- Bärlauchbrot (Wild Garlic Bread)
- Süßes Zopfgebäck (Sweet Braided Bread)
- Nussbrot (Nut Bread)
- Roggenbrot mit Honig (Rye Honey Bread)
- Vollkorn-Sauerteigbrot (Whole Grain Sourdough Bread)
- Schwarzbrot (Black Bread)
- Gurkenbrot (Cucumber Bread)
- Feigenbrot (Fig Bread)
- Krustenbrot (Crusty Bread)
- Wurzelbrot (Root Bread)
- Apfel-Zimt-Brot (Apple Cinnamon Bread)
- Schinkenbrot (Ham Bread)
- Sonnenblumen-Dinkelbrot (Sunflower Spelt Bread)
- Roggenbrot mit Kürbiskernen (Rye Bread with Pumpkin Seeds)
- Löwenzahn-Brot (Dandelion Bread)
- Butterbrot (Butter Bread)

Pumpernickel

Ingredients:

- **For the Soaker:**
    - 1 cup (240 ml) boiling water
    - 1 cup (150 g) coarsely ground rye flour
- **For the Dough:**
    - 1 cup (240 ml) warm water
    - 1 tablespoon (15 ml) molasses
    - 1 tablespoon (15 ml) honey
    - 2 teaspoons (10 g) salt
    - 1 ½ cups (225 g) coarsely ground rye flour
    - 1 ½ cups (225 g) finely ground rye flour
    - 1 tablespoon (10 g) active dry yeast
    - 1 tablespoon (15 g) caraway seeds (optional)
    - 1 tablespoon (15 g) cocoa powder (optional, for color)

Instructions:

1. **Prepare the Soaker:**
    - In a bowl, combine the boiling water and coarsely ground rye flour. Mix until smooth. Cover the bowl with plastic wrap and let it sit at room temperature for at least 8 hours or overnight.
2. **Prepare the Dough:**
    - In a large bowl, dissolve the yeast in warm water and let it sit for 5 minutes.
    - Add the molasses, honey, and salt to the yeast mixture and stir until well combined.
    - Mix in the soaker and then gradually add both types of rye flour, mixing until a sticky dough forms.
    - Stir in the caraway seeds and cocoa powder, if using.
3. **Knead and Rise:**
    - Turn the dough out onto a floured surface and knead for about 5-10 minutes, until it becomes smooth and elastic.
    - Place the dough in a greased bowl, cover with plastic wrap or a damp cloth, and let it rise in a warm place for about 1-1.5 hours, or until doubled in size.
4. **Shape and Bake:**
    - Preheat your oven to 350°F (175°C).
    - Punch down the dough and shape it into a loaf or place it into a greased loaf pan.
    - Cover and let it rise for an additional 30-45 minutes, until it has risen slightly.
    - Bake in the preheated oven for 45-60 minutes, or until the bread sounds hollow when tapped on the bottom and has a deep, dark brown color.
5. **Cool:**

- Allow the bread to cool in the pan for about 10 minutes before transferring it to a wire rack to cool completely.

Enjoy your homemade Pumpernickel bread! It pairs wonderfully with hearty cheeses and meats.

Rye Sourdough

Ingredients:

- **For the Sourdough Starter:**
    - ¼ cup (60 g) rye flour
    - ¼ cup (60 ml) water
    - 1 tablespoon (15 g) active rye sourdough starter (or a pinch of commercial yeast if starting from scratch)
- **For the Dough:**
    - 1 cup (240 ml) warm water
    - 1 cup (150 g) whole rye flour
    - 1 ½ cups (225 g) bread flour
    - 1 tablespoon (15 g) salt
    - 1 tablespoon (15 ml) honey (optional, for a touch of sweetness)
    - 1 cup (240 ml) active rye sourdough starter (prepared from the initial mixture)

Instructions:

1. **Prepare the Sourdough Starter:**
    - Mix the rye flour and water in a small bowl. Add the active rye sourdough starter if you have it; if starting from scratch, mix the flour and water, and let it sit at room temperature for 24 hours to begin fermenting.
    - After 24 hours, feed the starter with additional rye flour and water, and let it sit for another 24 hours. It should start bubbling and developing a sour smell.
2. **Prepare the Dough:**
    - In a large mixing bowl, combine the warm water and honey (if using).
    - Stir in the sourdough starter until well incorporated.
    - Gradually add the rye flour and bread flour, mixing until a shaggy dough forms.
    - Add the salt and mix until combined. The dough will be sticky and dense.
3. **First Rise:**
    - Cover the bowl with plastic wrap or a damp cloth and let the dough rise in a warm place for 4-6 hours, or until it has roughly doubled in size. It may not rise as much as wheat-based doughs, but it should show some increase in volume.
4. **Shape and Second Rise:**
    - Turn the dough out onto a lightly floured surface and shape it into a round or oval loaf. Place the shaped dough onto a parchment-lined or lightly greased baking sheet or into a floured proofing basket.
    - Cover with plastic wrap or a damp cloth and let it rise for another 1-2 hours, or until it has increased in size and looks puffy.
5. **Preheat Oven:**
    - Preheat your oven to 450°F (230°C). If using a baking stone, place it in the oven to preheat as well.

6. **Score and Bake:**
    - Using a sharp knife or a bread lame, make a few slashes on the surface of the dough to allow it to expand during baking.
    - Place the dough in the oven (on the preheated baking stone if using) and bake for 35-45 minutes, or until the loaf has a deep, dark brown crust and sounds hollow when tapped on the bottom.
7. **Cool:**
    - Remove the bread from the oven and cool on a wire rack for at least 1 hour before slicing.

Enjoy your homemade Rye Sourdough bread! It pairs wonderfully with soups, stews, and cheeses.

Weißbrot (White Bread)

Ingredients:

- 3 ½ cups (440 g) all-purpose flour
- 1 cup (240 ml) warm water (110°F or 45°C)
- 2 tablespoons (25 g) sugar
- 2 teaspoons (10 g) salt
- 2 teaspoons (6 g) active dry yeast
- 3 tablespoons (45 g) unsalted butter, softened
- 1 large egg
- 1 tablespoon (15 ml) milk (for brushing, optional)

Instructions:

1. **Prepare the Yeast:**
    - In a small bowl, dissolve the sugar in the warm water. Sprinkle the yeast over the surface and let it sit for 5-10 minutes, or until it becomes frothy and bubbly.
2. **Mix the Dough:**
    - In a large mixing bowl, combine the flour and salt.
    - Make a well in the center and add the yeast mixture, softened butter, and egg.
    - Stir with a wooden spoon or dough hook attachment until a rough dough forms.
3. **Knead the Dough:**
    - Turn the dough out onto a lightly floured surface and knead for about 8-10 minutes, or until it becomes smooth and elastic. Alternatively, you can use a stand mixer with a dough hook for about 5 minutes.
    - If the dough is too sticky, add a little more flour, a tablespoon at a time, until it's manageable.
4. **First Rise:**
    - Place the dough in a lightly greased bowl and cover it with plastic wrap or a damp cloth.
    - Let it rise in a warm place for about 1-1.5 hours, or until it has doubled in size.
5. **Shape the Dough:**
    - Punch down the risen dough to release air. Turn it out onto a lightly floured surface and shape it into a loaf.
    - Place the shaped dough into a greased 9x5 inch (23x13 cm) loaf pan or on a parchment-lined baking sheet if you prefer a free-form loaf.
6. **Second Rise:**
    - Cover the loaf with plastic wrap or a damp cloth and let it rise for another 30-45 minutes, or until it has risen above the edge of the pan.
7. **Preheat Oven:**
    - Preheat your oven to 375°F (190°C).
8. **Bake:**

- Brush the top of the loaf with milk, if desired, for a golden crust.
- Bake in the preheated oven for 25-30 minutes, or until the loaf is golden brown and sounds hollow when tapped on the bottom.

9. **Cool:**
    - Remove the bread from the oven and let it cool in the pan for 10 minutes.
    - Transfer to a wire rack to cool completely before slicing.

Enjoy your fresh, homemade Weißbrot! It's perfect for sandwiches, toasting, or simply enjoying with a bit of butter.

Kastenbrot (Loaf Bread)

Ingredients:

- 3 ½ cups (440 g) all-purpose flour
- 1 ½ cups (360 ml) warm water (110°F or 45°C)
- 2 tablespoons (25 g) sugar
- 2 teaspoons (10 g) salt
- 2 teaspoons (6 g) active dry yeast
- 3 tablespoons (45 g) unsalted butter, softened
- 1 large egg

Instructions:

1. **Prepare the Yeast:**
   - In a small bowl, dissolve the sugar in the warm water. Sprinkle the yeast over the surface and let it sit for 5-10 minutes, or until it becomes frothy and bubbly.
2. **Mix the Dough:**
   - In a large mixing bowl, combine the flour and salt.
   - Make a well in the center and add the yeast mixture, softened butter, and egg.
   - Stir with a wooden spoon or dough hook attachment until a rough dough forms.
3. **Knead the Dough:**
   - Turn the dough out onto a lightly floured surface and knead for about 8-10 minutes, or until it becomes smooth and elastic. Alternatively, you can use a stand mixer with a dough hook for about 5 minutes.
   - If the dough is too sticky, add a little more flour, a tablespoon at a time, until it's manageable.
4. **First Rise:**
   - Place the dough in a lightly greased bowl and cover it with plastic wrap or a damp cloth.
   - Let it rise in a warm place for about 1-1.5 hours, or until it has doubled in size.
5. **Shape the Dough:**
   - Punch down the risen dough to release air. Turn it out onto a lightly floured surface and shape it into a loaf.
   - Place the shaped dough into a greased 9x5 inch (23x13 cm) loaf pan. Press it down gently to fit the pan and smooth the top.
6. **Second Rise:**
   - Cover the loaf with plastic wrap or a damp cloth and let it rise for another 30-45 minutes, or until it has risen just above the edge of the pan.
7. **Preheat Oven:**
   - Preheat your oven to 375°F (190°C).
8. **Bake:**

- Bake in the preheated oven for 30-35 minutes, or until the loaf is golden brown and sounds hollow when tapped on the bottom.
9. **Cool:**
    - Remove the bread from the oven and let it cool in the pan for 10 minutes.
    - Transfer to a wire rack to cool completely before slicing.

Enjoy your homemade Kastenbrot! This loaf bread is great for sandwiches, toast, or just enjoying with a bit of butter.

Dinkelbrot (Spelt Bread)

Ingredients:

- **For the Dough:**
    - 3 ½ cups (440 g) spelt flour (whole or white spelt flour)
    - 1 ¼ cups (300 ml) warm water (110°F or 45°C)
    - 2 teaspoons (10 g) salt
    - 2 tablespoons (25 g) sugar or honey (optional, for a touch of sweetness)
    - 2 teaspoons (6 g) active dry yeast
    - 2 tablespoons (30 g) olive oil or melted butter
    - 1 tablespoon (15 ml) apple cider vinegar (for better texture, optional)
- **For the Optional Topping:**
    - 2 tablespoons (15 g) sunflower seeds or sesame seeds (optional)

Instructions:

1. **Prepare the Yeast:**
    - In a small bowl, dissolve the sugar or honey (if using) in the warm water. Sprinkle the yeast over the surface and let it sit for 5-10 minutes, or until it becomes frothy and bubbly.
2. **Mix the Dough:**
    - In a large mixing bowl, combine the spelt flour and salt.
    - Make a well in the center and add the yeast mixture, olive oil or melted butter, and apple cider vinegar (if using).
    - Stir until a rough dough forms.
3. **Knead the Dough:**
    - Turn the dough out onto a lightly floured surface and knead for about 8-10 minutes, or until it becomes smooth and elastic. Spelt dough may be slightly stickier than wheat dough, so add a little more flour if necessary.
    - Alternatively, you can use a stand mixer with a dough hook for about 5 minutes.
4. **First Rise:**
    - Place the dough in a lightly greased bowl and cover it with plastic wrap or a damp cloth.
    - Let it rise in a warm place for about 1-1.5 hours, or until it has doubled in size.
5. **Shape the Dough:**
    - Punch down the risen dough to release air. Turn it out onto a lightly floured surface and shape it into a loaf.
    - Place the shaped dough into a greased 9x5 inch (23x13 cm) loaf pan, or onto a parchment-lined baking sheet if you prefer a free-form loaf.
6. **Second Rise:**
    - Cover the loaf with plastic wrap or a damp cloth and let it rise for another 30-45 minutes, or until it has risen just above the edge of the pan.
7. **Preheat Oven:**
    - Preheat your oven to 375°F (190°C).
8. **Add Toppings:**
    - If using, sprinkle sunflower seeds or sesame seeds on top of the loaf.

9. **Bake:**
    - Bake in the preheated oven for 30-35 minutes, or until the loaf is golden brown and sounds hollow when tapped on the bottom.
10. **Cool:**
    - Remove the bread from the oven and let it cool in the pan for 10 minutes.
    - Transfer to a wire rack to cool completely before slicing.

Enjoy your homemade Dinkelbrot! Spelt bread has a slightly nutty flavor and a great texture, making it a delightful option for sandwiches or toast.

Sonnenblumenbrot (Sunflower Seed Bread)

Ingredients:

- **For the Dough:**
    - 3 ½ cups (440 g) all-purpose or bread flour
    - 1 cup (150 g) whole wheat flour
    - 1 cup (240 ml) warm water (110°F or 45°C)
    - 2 teaspoons (6 g) active dry yeast
    - 2 tablespoons (25 g) sugar or honey
    - 2 teaspoons (10 g) salt
    - 2 tablespoons (30 ml) olive oil
    - ½ cup (80 g) sunflower seeds (plus extra for topping)
    - 2 tablespoons (15 g) flaxseeds (optional, for added nutrition and texture)

Instructions:

1. **Prepare the Yeast:**
    - In a small bowl, dissolve the sugar or honey in the warm water. Sprinkle the yeast over the surface and let it sit for 5-10 minutes, or until it becomes frothy and bubbly.
2. **Mix the Dough:**
    - In a large mixing bowl, combine the all-purpose or bread flour, whole wheat flour, and salt.
    - Make a well in the center and add the yeast mixture and olive oil.
    - Stir until a rough dough forms, then fold in the sunflower seeds and flaxseeds if using.
3. **Knead the Dough:**
    - Turn the dough out onto a lightly floured surface and knead for about 8-10 minutes, or until it becomes smooth and elastic. Alternatively, you can use a stand mixer with a dough hook for about 5 minutes.
4. **First Rise:**
    - Place the dough in a lightly greased bowl and cover it with plastic wrap or a damp cloth.
    - Let it rise in a warm place for about 1-1.5 hours, or until it has doubled in size.
5. **Shape the Dough:**
    - Punch down the risen dough to release air. Turn it out onto a lightly floured surface and shape it into a loaf or divide it into smaller portions for rolls.
    - Place the shaped dough into a greased 9x5 inch (23x13 cm) loaf pan or onto a parchment-lined baking sheet if making rolls.
6. **Second Rise:**

- Cover the loaf or rolls with plastic wrap or a damp cloth and let them rise for another 30-45 minutes, or until they have risen just above the edge of the pan or are puffy.
7. **Preheat Oven:**
    - Preheat your oven to 375°F (190°C).
8. **Add Toppings:**
    - If desired, brush the top of the loaf or rolls with a little water or milk and sprinkle with additional sunflower seeds for a crunchy topping.
9. **Bake:**
    - Bake in the preheated oven for 30-35 minutes for a loaf, or 20-25 minutes for rolls, until golden brown and sounding hollow when tapped on the bottom.
10. **Cool:**
    - Remove from the oven and let the bread cool in the pan for 10 minutes before transferring to a wire rack to cool completely.

Enjoy your homemade Sonnenblumenbrot! This bread has a delightful crunch from the sunflower seeds and is perfect for sandwiches, toast, or simply enjoying with a bit of butter.

Bauernbrot (Farmer's Bread)

Ingredients:

- **For the Dough:**
    - 3 ½ cups (440 g) all-purpose or bread flour
    - 1 ½ cups (225 g) whole wheat flour
    - 1 ¼ cups (300 ml) warm water (110°F or 45°C)
    - 1 tablespoon (15 g) sugar or honey
    - 2 teaspoons (10 g) salt
    - 2 teaspoons (6 g) active dry yeast
    - 2 tablespoons (30 ml) olive oil or melted butter
- **For the Starter (optional, for enhanced flavor):**
    - ¼ cup (60 g) whole wheat flour
    - ¼ cup (60 ml) warm water
    - 1 tablespoon (15 g) sourdough starter or ¼ teaspoon of active dry yeast

Instructions:

1. **Prepare the Starter (Optional):**
    - In a small bowl, combine the whole wheat flour and warm water. Add the sourdough starter or yeast. Mix well and let it sit at room temperature for about 8 hours or overnight. This step enhances the flavor but can be skipped if you're short on time.
2. **Prepare the Yeast:**
    - If not using the starter, dissolve the sugar in the warm water. Sprinkle the yeast over the surface and let it sit for 5-10 minutes, or until it becomes frothy and bubbly.
3. **Mix the Dough:**
    - In a large mixing bowl, combine the all-purpose or bread flour, whole wheat flour, and salt.
    - Make a well in the center and add the yeast mixture (or the starter mixture if using), and olive oil or melted butter.
    - Stir until a rough dough forms.
4. **Knead the Dough:**
    - Turn the dough out onto a lightly floured surface and knead for about 8-10 minutes, or until it becomes smooth and elastic. Alternatively, use a stand mixer with a dough hook for about 5 minutes.
5. **First Rise:**
    - Place the dough in a lightly greased bowl and cover it with plastic wrap or a damp cloth.
    - Let it rise in a warm place for about 1-1.5 hours, or until it has doubled in size.
6. **Shape the Dough:**

- Punch down the risen dough to release air. Turn it out onto a lightly floured surface and shape it into a round or oval loaf.
- Place the shaped dough onto a parchment-lined baking sheet or into a greased 9x5 inch (23x13 cm) loaf pan if preferred.

7. **Second Rise:**
    - Cover the loaf with plastic wrap or a damp cloth and let it rise for another 30-45 minutes, or until it has risen just above the edge of the pan or is puffy.
8. **Preheat Oven:**
    - Preheat your oven to 375°F (190°C).
9. **Bake:**
    - For a crustier loaf, make a few shallow slashes on the top of the dough with a sharp knife or bread lame.
    - Bake in the preheated oven for 30-35 minutes, or until the loaf is golden brown and sounds hollow when tapped on the bottom.
10. **Cool:**
    - Remove from the oven and let the bread cool in the pan for 10 minutes before transferring it to a wire rack to cool completely.

Enjoy your homemade Bauernbrot! This hearty bread is perfect for sandwiches, soups, or simply enjoyed with butter and cheese.

Roggenmischbrot (Rye and Wheat Bread)

Ingredients:

- **For the Dough:**
    - 2 cups (250 g) rye flour
    - 2 cups (250 g) all-purpose or bread flour
    - 1 ¼ cups (300 ml) warm water (110°F or 45°C)
    - 1 tablespoon (15 g) sugar or honey
    - 2 teaspoons (10 g) salt
    - 2 teaspoons (6 g) active dry yeast
    - 2 tablespoons (30 ml) olive oil or melted butter
    - 1 tablespoon (15 ml) apple cider vinegar (optional, for better texture)
- **For the Starter (optional, for enhanced flavor):**
    - ½ cup (60 g) rye flour
    - ½ cup (120 ml) warm water
    - 1 tablespoon (15 g) sourdough starter or ¼ teaspoon of active dry yeast

Instructions:

1. **Prepare the Starter (Optional):**
    - In a small bowl, mix the rye flour and warm water. Add the sourdough starter or yeast. Mix well and let it sit at room temperature for about 8 hours or overnight. This step enhances the flavor but can be skipped if you're short on time.
2. **Prepare the Yeast:**
    - If not using the starter, dissolve the sugar in the warm water. Sprinkle the yeast over the surface and let it sit for 5-10 minutes, or until it becomes frothy and bubbly.
3. **Mix the Dough:**
    - In a large mixing bowl, combine the rye flour, all-purpose or bread flour, and salt.
    - Make a well in the center and add the yeast mixture (or the starter mixture if using), olive oil or melted butter, and apple cider vinegar (if using).
    - Stir until a rough dough forms.
4. **Knead the Dough:**
    - Turn the dough out onto a lightly floured surface and knead for about 8-10 minutes, or until it becomes smooth and elastic. Alternatively, use a stand mixer with a dough hook for about 5 minutes.
5. **First Rise:**
    - Place the dough in a lightly greased bowl and cover it with plastic wrap or a damp cloth.
    - Let it rise in a warm place for about 1-1.5 hours, or until it has doubled in size.
6. **Shape the Dough:**

- Punch down the risen dough to release air. Turn it out onto a lightly floured surface and shape it into a loaf or divide it into smaller portions if making rolls.
- Place the shaped dough into a greased 9x5 inch (23x13 cm) loaf pan or onto a parchment-lined baking sheet if making rolls.

7. **Second Rise:**
   - Cover the loaf or rolls with plastic wrap or a damp cloth and let them rise for another 30-45 minutes, or until they have risen just above the edge of the pan or are puffy.
8. **Preheat Oven:**
   - Preheat your oven to 375°F (190°C).
9. **Bake:**
   - For a crustier loaf, make a few shallow slashes on the top of the dough with a sharp knife or bread lame.
   - Bake in the preheated oven for 30-35 minutes for a loaf, or 20-25 minutes for rolls, until golden brown and sounding hollow when tapped on the bottom.
10. **Cool:**
    - Remove from the oven and let the bread cool in the pan for 10 minutes before transferring it to a wire rack to cool completely.

Enjoy your homemade Roggenmischbrot! This bread has a hearty flavor with a nice balance of rye and wheat, perfect for sandwiches or served with a variety of spreads.

Zwiebelbrot (Onion Bread)

Ingredients:

- **For the Dough:**
    - 3 ½ cups (440 g) all-purpose flour
    - 1 cup (150 g) whole wheat flour (optional, for added texture and flavor)
    - 1 ¼ cups (300 ml) warm water (110°F or 45°C)
    - 2 teaspoons (6 g) active dry yeast
    - 1 tablespoon (15 g) sugar or honey
    - 2 teaspoons (10 g) salt
    - 2 tablespoons (30 ml) olive oil or melted butter
    - 1 tablespoon (15 ml) apple cider vinegar (optional, for better texture)
- **For the Onion Filling:**
    - 1 large onion, finely chopped
    - 2 tablespoons (30 ml) olive oil
    - 1 teaspoon (5 g) sugar (to caramelize the onions)
    - 1 teaspoon (5 g) dried thyme or rosemary (optional, for added flavor)
    - Salt and pepper to taste

Instructions:

1. **Prepare the Onion Filling:**
    - Heat the olive oil in a skillet over medium heat.
    - Add the chopped onion and cook, stirring occasionally, until the onions are soft and golden brown, about 10-15 minutes.
    - Add the sugar and continue cooking until the onions are caramelized, about 5 more minutes.
    - Season with salt, pepper, and dried thyme or rosemary if using. Remove from heat and let it cool slightly.
2. **Prepare the Yeast:**
    - In a small bowl, dissolve the sugar or honey in the warm water. Sprinkle the yeast over the surface and let it sit for 5-10 minutes, or until it becomes frothy and bubbly.
3. **Mix the Dough:**
    - In a large mixing bowl, combine the all-purpose flour, whole wheat flour (if using), and salt.
    - Make a well in the center and add the yeast mixture, olive oil or melted butter, and apple cider vinegar (if using).
    - Stir until a rough dough forms.
4. **Knead the Dough:**

- Turn the dough out onto a lightly floured surface and knead for about 8-10 minutes, or until it becomes smooth and elastic. Alternatively, use a stand mixer with a dough hook for about 5 minutes.

5. **Incorporate the Onions:**
   - Gently fold the cooled caramelized onions into the dough, being careful not to overwork it.
6. **First Rise:**
   - Place the dough in a lightly greased bowl and cover it with plastic wrap or a damp cloth.
   - Let it rise in a warm place for about 1-1.5 hours, or until it has doubled in size.
7. **Shape the Dough:**
   - Punch down the risen dough to release air. Turn it out onto a lightly floured surface and shape it into a loaf or divide it into smaller portions if making rolls.
   - Place the shaped dough into a greased 9x5 inch (23x13 cm) loaf pan or onto a parchment-lined baking sheet if making rolls.
8. **Second Rise:**
   - Cover the loaf or rolls with plastic wrap or a damp cloth and let them rise for another 30-45 minutes, or until they have risen just above the edge of the pan or are puffy.
9. **Preheat Oven:**
   - Preheat your oven to 375°F (190°C).
10. **Bake:**
    - For a crustier loaf, make a few shallow slashes on the top of the dough with a sharp knife or bread lame.
    - Bake in the preheated oven for 30-35 minutes for a loaf, or 20-25 minutes for rolls, until golden brown and sounding hollow when tapped on the bottom.
11. **Cool:**
    - Remove from the oven and let the bread cool in the pan for 10 minutes before transferring it to a wire rack to cool completely.

Enjoy your homemade Zwiebelbrot! The caramelized onions add a wonderful depth of flavor to this bread, making it perfect for sandwiches, toasted with cheese, or served alongside soups and stews.

Körnerbrot (Seed Bread)

Ingredients:

- **For the Dough:**
    - 3 ½ cups (440 g) all-purpose or bread flour
    - 1 cup (150 g) whole wheat flour (optional, for added texture and flavor)
    - 1 ¼ cups (300 ml) warm water (110°F or 45°C)
    - 2 teaspoons (6 g) active dry yeast
    - 1 tablespoon (15 g) sugar or honey
    - 2 teaspoons (10 g) salt
    - 2 tablespoons (30 ml) olive oil or melted butter
    - 1 tablespoon (15 ml) apple cider vinegar (optional, for better texture)
- **For the Seed Mixture:**
    - ¼ cup (40 g) sunflower seeds
    - ¼ cup (40 g) sesame seeds
    - ¼ cup (40 g) pumpkin seeds
    - 2 tablespoons (20 g) flaxseeds (optional)
    - 2 tablespoons (20 g) chia seeds (optional)

Instructions:

1. **Prepare the Yeast:**
    - In a small bowl, dissolve the sugar or honey in the warm water. Sprinkle the yeast over the surface and let it sit for 5-10 minutes, or until it becomes frothy and bubbly.
2. **Mix the Dough:**
    - In a large mixing bowl, combine the all-purpose or bread flour, whole wheat flour (if using), and salt.
    - Make a well in the center and add the yeast mixture, olive oil or melted butter, and apple cider vinegar (if using).
    - Stir until a rough dough forms.
3. **Incorporate the Seeds:**
    - Gently fold the seed mixture into the dough until evenly distributed.
4. **Knead the Dough:**
    - Turn the dough out onto a lightly floured surface and knead for about 8-10 minutes, or until it becomes smooth and elastic. Alternatively, use a stand mixer with a dough hook for about 5 minutes.
5. **First Rise:**
    - Place the dough in a lightly greased bowl and cover it with plastic wrap or a damp cloth.
    - Let it rise in a warm place for about 1-1.5 hours, or until it has doubled in size.
6. **Shape the Dough:**

- Punch down the risen dough to release air. Turn it out onto a lightly floured surface and shape it into a loaf or divide it into smaller portions if making rolls.
- Place the shaped dough into a greased 9x5 inch (23x13 cm) loaf pan or onto a parchment-lined baking sheet if making rolls.

7. **Second Rise:**
    - Cover the loaf or rolls with plastic wrap or a damp cloth and let them rise for another 30-45 minutes, or until they have risen just above the edge of the pan or are puffy.
8. **Preheat Oven:**
    - Preheat your oven to 375°F (190°C).
9. **Add Toppings:**
    - If desired, sprinkle additional seeds on top of the loaf or rolls before baking.
10. **Bake:**
    - Bake in the preheated oven for 30-35 minutes for a loaf, or 20-25 minutes for rolls, until golden brown and sounding hollow when tapped on the bottom.
11. **Cool:**
    - Remove from the oven and let the bread cool in the pan for 10 minutes before transferring it to a wire rack to cool completely.

Enjoy your homemade Körnerbrot! This hearty, seed-packed bread is perfect for sandwiches, toasting, or as a nutritious addition to any meal.

Bierbrot (Beer Bread)

Ingredients:

- 3 cups (375 g) all-purpose flour
- 1/4 cup (50 g) sugar
- 1 tablespoon (15 g) baking powder
- 1 teaspoon (5 g) salt
- 1/2 cup (115 g) unsalted butter, melted
- 1 bottle (12 oz or 355 ml) of beer (any type you prefer, but a pale ale or lager works well)
- 1 large egg (optional, for added richness)
- 1 tablespoon (15 ml) honey or molasses (optional, for extra sweetness)

Instructions:

1. **Preheat Oven:**
    - Preheat your oven to 375°F (190°C).
2. **Prepare the Dry Ingredients:**
    - In a large mixing bowl, whisk together the flour, sugar, baking powder, and salt.
3. **Combine Wet Ingredients:**
    - In a separate bowl, mix the melted butter with the beer. If using, add the egg and honey or molasses to the butter and beer mixture and whisk to combine.
4. **Mix the Dough:**
    - Pour the wet ingredients into the dry ingredients. Stir gently until just combined. The batter will be thick and lumpy, which is normal. Be careful not to overmix.
5. **Pour into Pan:**
    - Pour the batter into a greased 9x5 inch (23x13 cm) loaf pan, smoothing the top with a spatula.
6. **Bake:**
    - Bake in the preheated oven for 45-50 minutes, or until the top is golden brown and a toothpick inserted into the center comes out clean.
7. **Cool:**
    - Allow the bread to cool in the pan for 10 minutes, then transfer to a wire rack to cool completely before slicing.

Enjoy your homemade Bierbrot! This bread has a lovely, malty flavor from the beer and pairs well with a variety of dishes or simply enjoyed with a pat of butter.

Laugenbrötchen (Pretzel Rolls)

Ingredients:

- **For the Dough:**
    - 3 ½ cups (440 g) all-purpose flour
    - 1 cup (150 g) whole wheat flour (optional, for added texture and flavor)
    - 1 ¼ cups (300 ml) warm water (110°F or 45°C)
    - 2 teaspoons (6 g) active dry yeast
    - 1 tablespoon (15 g) sugar
    - 1 teaspoon (5 g) salt
    - 2 tablespoons (30 ml) unsalted butter, softened
- **For the Baking Soda Bath:**
    - 4 cups (1 liter) water
    - ¼ cup (60 g) baking soda
- **For the Topping:**
    - Coarse sea salt

Instructions:

1. **Prepare the Yeast:**
    - In a small bowl, dissolve the sugar in the warm water. Sprinkle the yeast over the surface and let it sit for 5-10 minutes, or until it becomes frothy and bubbly.
2. **Mix the Dough:**
    - In a large mixing bowl, combine the all-purpose flour, whole wheat flour (if using), and salt.
    - Make a well in the center and add the yeast mixture and softened butter.
    - Stir until a rough dough forms.
3. **Knead the Dough:**
    - Turn the dough out onto a lightly floured surface and knead for about 8-10 minutes, or until it becomes smooth and elastic. Alternatively, use a stand mixer with a dough hook for about 5 minutes.
4. **First Rise:**
    - Place the dough in a lightly greased bowl and cover it with plastic wrap or a damp cloth.
    - Let it rise in a warm place for about 1-1.5 hours, or until it has doubled in size.
5. **Shape the Rolls:**
    - Punch down the risen dough to release air. Turn it out onto a lightly floured surface and divide it into 8-12 equal pieces.
    - Shape each piece into a ball and place them on a parchment-lined baking sheet. If you prefer, you can also shape them into oval rolls.
6. **Second Rise:**

- Cover the rolls with plastic wrap or a damp cloth and let them rise for another 30 minutes.
7. **Prepare the Baking Soda Bath:**
    - In a large pot, bring 4 cups of water to a boil. Carefully add the baking soda, stirring to dissolve.
    - Reduce the heat to a simmer.
8. **Boil the Rolls:**
    - Using a slotted spoon or spatula, carefully lower a few rolls into the simmering baking soda bath. Boil for about 30 seconds, then flip and boil for another 30 seconds.
    - Remove the rolls and place them back on the parchment-lined baking sheet. Repeat with the remaining rolls.
9. **Add Toppings:**
    - While the rolls are still wet from the baking soda bath, sprinkle them with coarse sea salt.
10. **Preheat Oven:**
    - Preheat your oven to 425°F (220°C).
11. **Bake:**
    - Bake the rolls in the preheated oven for 15-20 minutes, or until they are deep brown and sound hollow when tapped on the bottom.
12. **Cool:**
    - Remove the rolls from the oven and let them cool on a wire rack.

Enjoy your homemade Laugenbrötchen! These pretzel rolls are great with butter, as a sandwich base, or served with soups and stews.

Rosinenbrot (Raisin Bread)

Ingredients:

- **For the Dough:**
    - 3 ½ cups (440 g) all-purpose flour
    - ¼ cup (50 g) sugar
    - 1 teaspoon (5 g) salt
    - 2 teaspoons (6 g) active dry yeast
    - 1 cup (240 ml) warm milk (110°F or 45°C)
    - ¼ cup (60 g) unsalted butter, softened
    - 1 large egg
    - 1 teaspoon (5 g) ground cinnamon
    - ¼ teaspoon (1 g) ground nutmeg (optional)
    - 1 cup (150 g) raisins (or more if desired)
- **For the Glaze (optional):**
    - 2 tablespoons (25 g) sugar
    - 2 tablespoons (30 ml) water

Instructions:

1. **Prepare the Yeast:**
    - In a small bowl, dissolve 1 tablespoon of the sugar in the warm milk. Sprinkle the yeast over the surface and let it sit for 5-10 minutes, or until it becomes frothy and bubbly.
2. **Mix the Dough:**
    - In a large mixing bowl, combine the flour, remaining sugar, salt, cinnamon, and nutmeg if using.
    - Make a well in the center and add the yeast mixture, softened butter, and egg.
    - Stir until a rough dough forms.
3. **Knead the Dough:**
    - Turn the dough out onto a lightly floured surface and knead for about 8-10 minutes, or until it becomes smooth and elastic. Alternatively, use a stand mixer with a dough hook for about 5 minutes.
4. **Incorporate the Raisins:**
    - Gently fold the raisins into the dough until evenly distributed.
5. **First Rise:**
    - Place the dough in a lightly greased bowl and cover it with plastic wrap or a damp cloth.
    - Let it rise in a warm place for about 1-1.5 hours, or until it has doubled in size.
6. **Shape the Bread:**
    - Punch down the risen dough to release air. Turn it out onto a lightly floured surface and shape it into a loaf.

- Place the shaped dough into a greased 9x5 inch (23x13 cm) loaf pan.
7. **Second Rise:**
    - Cover the loaf with plastic wrap or a damp cloth and let it rise for another 30-45 minutes, or until it has risen just above the edge of the pan.
8. **Preheat Oven:**
    - Preheat your oven to 375°F (190°C).
9. **Bake:**
    - Bake in the preheated oven for 30-35 minutes, or until the loaf is golden brown and sounds hollow when tapped on the bottom.
10. **Prepare the Glaze (Optional):**
    - While the bread is baking, you can prepare the glaze by combining sugar and water in a small saucepan. Heat over medium heat until the sugar dissolves, then remove from heat.
11. **Cool and Glaze:**
    - Remove the bread from the oven and immediately brush the top with the sugar glaze, if using.
    - Let the bread cool in the pan for 10 minutes, then transfer to a wire rack to cool completely.

Enjoy your homemade Rosinenbrot! This sweet, raisin-studded bread is perfect on its own or toasted with a bit of butter.

Käsebrot (Cheese Bread)

Ingredients:

- **For the Dough:**
    - 3 ½ cups (440 g) all-purpose flour
    - 1 cup (150 g) shredded cheese (such as cheddar, gouda, or a blend)
    - 1 cup (240 ml) warm milk (110°F or 45°C)
    - 2 teaspoons (6 g) active dry yeast
    - 2 tablespoons (30 g) sugar
    - 1 teaspoon (5 g) salt
    - ¼ cup (60 g) unsalted butter, softened
    - 1 large egg
- **For the Cheese Topping:**
    - ½ cup (50 g) shredded cheese (matching the type used in the dough)
    - 1 tablespoon (15 g) grated Parmesan cheese (optional, for extra flavor)

Instructions:

1. **Prepare the Yeast:**
    - In a small bowl, dissolve the sugar in the warm milk. Sprinkle the yeast over the surface and let it sit for 5-10 minutes, or until it becomes frothy and bubbly.
2. **Mix the Dough:**
    - In a large mixing bowl, combine the flour and salt.
    - Make a well in the center and add the yeast mixture, softened butter, and egg.
    - Stir until a rough dough forms.
3. **Incorporate the Cheese:**
    - Gently fold in the shredded cheese until evenly distributed.
4. **Knead the Dough:**
    - Turn the dough out onto a lightly floured surface and knead for about 8-10 minutes, or until it becomes smooth and elastic. Alternatively, use a stand mixer with a dough hook for about 5 minutes.
5. **First Rise:**
    - Place the dough in a lightly greased bowl and cover it with plastic wrap or a damp cloth.
    - Let it rise in a warm place for about 1-1.5 hours, or until it has doubled in size.
6. **Shape the Bread:**
    - Punch down the risen dough to release air. Turn it out onto a lightly floured surface and shape it into a loaf.
    - Place the shaped dough into a greased 9x5 inch (23x13 cm) loaf pan.
7. **Second Rise:**
    - Cover the loaf with plastic wrap or a damp cloth and let it rise for another 30-45 minutes, or until it has risen just above the edge of the pan.

8. **Preheat Oven:**
   - Preheat your oven to 375°F (190°C).
9. **Add Toppings:**
   - Sprinkle the top of the loaf with additional shredded cheese and Parmesan cheese if using.
10. **Bake:**
    - Bake in the preheated oven for 30-35 minutes, or until the loaf is golden brown and sounds hollow when tapped on the bottom.
11. **Cool:**
    - Remove the bread from the oven and let it cool in the pan for 10 minutes before transferring it to a wire rack to cool completely.

Enjoy your homemade Käsebrot! This cheesy bread is delicious on its own or served with a variety of dishes. It's especially great for dipping into soups or enjoying as a sandwich.

Kürbiskernbrot (Pumpkin Seed Bread)

Ingredients:

- **For the Dough:**
    - 3 cups (375 g) all-purpose or bread flour
    - 1 cup (125 g) whole wheat flour (optional, for added texture and flavor)
    - 1 ¼ cups (300 ml) warm water (110°F or 45°C)
    - 2 teaspoons (6 g) active dry yeast
    - 1 tablespoon (15 g) sugar or honey
    - 2 teaspoons (10 g) salt
    - 2 tablespoons (30 ml) olive oil or melted butter
    - 1 tablespoon (15 ml) apple cider vinegar (optional, for better texture)
- **For the Pumpkin Seed Mixture:**
    - ½ cup (60 g) pumpkin seeds (plus extra for topping)

Instructions:

1. **Prepare the Yeast:**
    - In a small bowl, dissolve the sugar or honey in the warm water. Sprinkle the yeast over the surface and let it sit for 5-10 minutes, or until it becomes frothy and bubbly.
2. **Mix the Dough:**
    - In a large mixing bowl, combine the all-purpose flour, whole wheat flour (if using), and salt.
    - Make a well in the center and add the yeast mixture, olive oil or melted butter, and apple cider vinegar (if using).
    - Stir until a rough dough forms.
3. **Incorporate the Pumpkin Seeds:**
    - Gently fold the pumpkin seeds into the dough until evenly distributed.
4. **Knead the Dough:**
    - Turn the dough out onto a lightly floured surface and knead for about 8-10 minutes, or until it becomes smooth and elastic. Alternatively, use a stand mixer with a dough hook for about 5 minutes.
5. **First Rise:**
    - Place the dough in a lightly greased bowl and cover it with plastic wrap or a damp cloth.
    - Let it rise in a warm place for about 1-1.5 hours, or until it has doubled in size.
6. **Shape the Bread:**
    - Punch down the risen dough to release air. Turn it out onto a lightly floured surface and shape it into a loaf.
    - Place the shaped dough into a greased 9x5 inch (23x13 cm) loaf pan or onto a parchment-lined baking sheet if making a round loaf.

7. **Second Rise:**
   - Cover the loaf with plastic wrap or a damp cloth and let it rise for another 30-45 minutes, or until it has risen just above the edge of the pan or is puffy.
8. **Preheat Oven:**
   - Preheat your oven to 375°F (190°C).
9. **Add Toppings:**
   - If desired, sprinkle additional pumpkin seeds on top of the loaf before baking.
10. **Bake:**
    - Bake in the preheated oven for 30-35 minutes, or until the loaf is golden brown and sounds hollow when tapped on the bottom.
11. **Cool:**
    - Remove the bread from the oven and let it cool in the pan for 10 minutes before transferring it to a wire rack to cool completely.

Enjoy your homemade Kürbiskernbrot! The pumpkin seeds add a wonderful crunch and nutty flavor to this bread, making it a great choice for sandwiches, toast, or simply enjoyed with a bit of butter.

Sauerteigbrot (Sourdough Bread)

Ingredients:

- **For the Starter:**
    - ¼ cup (60 g) active sourdough starter (fed and bubbly)
    - ½ cup (120 ml) warm water (110°F or 45°C)
    - ½ cup (60 g) all-purpose or bread flour
- **For the Dough:**
    - 1 ½ cups (360 ml) warm water (110°F or 45°C)
    - 3 ½ cups (440 g) all-purpose or bread flour
    - 2 teaspoons (10 g) salt
    - 1 tablespoon (15 g) sugar or honey (optional, for a slightly sweeter dough)
    - 1 cup (240 g) sourdough starter (active and bubbly)

Instructions:

1. **Prepare the Starter:**
    - In a small bowl, mix the sourdough starter, warm water, and flour. Cover and let it sit at room temperature for about 8-12 hours, or until bubbly and active. This step is typically done the night before you plan to bake.
2. **Mix the Dough:**
    - In a large mixing bowl, combine the flour and salt.
    - Make a well in the center and add the warm water, sourdough starter, and sugar or honey if using.
    - Stir until a rough dough forms.
3. **Knead the Dough:**
    - Turn the dough out onto a lightly floured surface and knead for about 8-10 minutes, or until it becomes smooth and elastic. Alternatively, use a stand mixer with a dough hook for about 5 minutes.
4. **First Rise:**
    - Place the dough in a lightly greased bowl and cover it with plastic wrap or a damp cloth.
    - Let it rise in a warm place for about 4-6 hours, or until it has doubled in size. This time can vary based on the strength of your starter and ambient temperature.
5. **Shape the Dough:**
    - Punch down the risen dough to release air. Turn it out onto a lightly floured surface and shape it into a loaf or divide it into smaller portions if making rolls.
    - Place the shaped dough into a greased 9x5 inch (23x13 cm) loaf pan or onto a parchment-lined baking sheet if making a round loaf.
6. **Second Rise:**
    - Cover the loaf with plastic wrap or a damp cloth and let it rise for another 1-2 hours, or until it has risen just above the edge of the pan or is puffy.

7. **Preheat Oven:**
   - Preheat your oven to 450°F (230°C).
8. **Bake:**
   - For a crustier loaf, make a few shallow slashes on the top of the dough with a sharp knife or bread lame.
   - Bake in the preheated oven for 30-35 minutes, or until the loaf is deep golden brown and sounds hollow when tapped on the bottom.
9. **Cool:**
   - Remove the bread from the oven and let it cool in the pan for 10 minutes before transferring it to a wire rack to cool completely.

Enjoy your homemade Sauerteigbrot! This sourdough bread has a delightful tangy flavor and a satisfying crust. It's perfect for sandwiches, toast, or simply enjoyed with a bit of butter.

Vollkornbrot (Whole Grain Bread)

Ingredients:

- **For the Dough:**
  - 2 ½ cups (310 g) whole wheat flour
  - 1 cup (125 g) all-purpose flour
  - 1 ¼ cups (300 ml) warm water (110°F or 45°C)
  - 2 teaspoons (6 g) active dry yeast
  - 1 tablespoon (15 g) honey or maple syrup
  - 1 teaspoon (5 g) salt
  - ¼ cup (30 ml) vegetable oil or melted butter
  - 1 tablespoon (15 ml) apple cider vinegar (optional, for better texture)
- **For the Add-ins (optional):**
  - ½ cup (80 g) sunflower seeds
  - ¼ cup (40 g) flaxseeds
  - ¼ cup (40 g) pumpkin seeds
  - ¼ cup (40 g) chopped nuts (such as walnuts or almonds)

Instructions:

1. **Prepare the Yeast:**
   - In a small bowl, dissolve the honey or maple syrup in the warm water. Sprinkle the yeast over the surface and let it sit for 5-10 minutes, or until it becomes frothy and bubbly.
2. **Mix the Dough:**
   - In a large mixing bowl, combine the whole wheat flour, all-purpose flour, and salt.
   - Make a well in the center and add the yeast mixture, vegetable oil or melted butter, and apple cider vinegar if using.
   - Stir until a rough dough forms.
3. **Incorporate the Add-ins (if using):**
   - Gently fold in the sunflower seeds, flaxseeds, pumpkin seeds, and nuts until evenly distributed.
4. **Knead the Dough:**
   - Turn the dough out onto a lightly floured surface and knead for about 8-10 minutes, or until it becomes smooth and elastic. Alternatively, use a stand mixer with a dough hook for about 5 minutes.
5. **First Rise:**
   - Place the dough in a lightly greased bowl and cover it with plastic wrap or a damp cloth.
   - Let it rise in a warm place for about 1-1.5 hours, or until it has doubled in size.
6. **Shape the Bread:**
   - Punch down the risen dough to release air. Turn it out onto a lightly floured surface and shape it into a loaf.
   - Place the shaped dough into a greased 9x5 inch (23x13 cm) loaf pan or onto a parchment-lined baking sheet if making a free-form loaf.
7. **Second Rise:**

- Cover the loaf with plastic wrap or a damp cloth and let it rise for another 30-45 minutes, or until it has risen just above the edge of the pan or is puffy.
8. **Preheat Oven:**
    - Preheat your oven to 375°F (190°C).
9. **Bake:**
    - Bake in the preheated oven for 30-35 minutes, or until the loaf is golden brown and sounds hollow when tapped on the bottom.
10. **Cool:**
    - Remove the bread from the oven and let it cool in the pan for 10 minutes before transferring it to a wire rack to cool completely.

Enjoy your homemade Vollkornbrot! This whole grain bread is packed with flavor and nutrients, making it a great choice for sandwiches, toasts, or simply enjoying with a bit of butter or your favorite spread.

Dreikornbrot (Three-Grain Bread)

Ingredients:

- **For the Dough:**
    - 1 cup (120 g) rye flour
    - 1 cup (120 g) whole wheat flour
    - 1 cup (120 g) all-purpose or bread flour
    - 1 ½ cups (360 ml) warm water (110°F or 45°C)
    - 2 teaspoons (6 g) active dry yeast
    - 1 tablespoon (15 g) honey or molasses
    - 1 teaspoon (5 g) salt
    - ¼ cup (30 ml) vegetable oil or melted butter
- **For the Seed Mixture (optional):**
    - ¼ cup (30 g) sunflower seeds
    - ¼ cup (30 g) pumpkin seeds
    - ¼ cup (30 g) flaxseeds

Instructions:

1. **Prepare the Yeast:**
    - In a small bowl, dissolve the honey or molasses in the warm water. Sprinkle the yeast over the surface and let it sit for 5-10 minutes, or until it becomes frothy and bubbly.
2. **Mix the Dough:**
    - In a large mixing bowl, combine the rye flour, whole wheat flour, and all-purpose flour.
    - Make a well in the center and add the yeast mixture, vegetable oil or melted butter, and salt.
    - Stir until a rough dough forms.
3. **Incorporate the Seeds (if using):**
    - Gently fold in the sunflower seeds, pumpkin seeds, and flaxseeds until evenly distributed.
4. **Knead the Dough:**
    - Turn the dough out onto a lightly floured surface and knead for about 8-10 minutes, or until it becomes smooth and elastic. Alternatively, use a stand mixer with a dough hook for about 5 minutes.
5. **First Rise:**
    - Place the dough in a lightly greased bowl and cover it with plastic wrap or a damp cloth.
    - Let it rise in a warm place for about 1-1.5 hours, or until it has doubled in size.
6. **Shape the Bread:**

- Punch down the risen dough to release air. Turn it out onto a lightly floured surface and shape it into a loaf.
- Place the shaped dough into a greased 9x5 inch (23x13 cm) loaf pan or onto a parchment-lined baking sheet if making a free-form loaf.

7. **Second Rise:**
    - Cover the loaf with plastic wrap or a damp cloth and let it rise for another 30-45 minutes, or until it has risen just above the edge of the pan or is puffy.
8. **Preheat Oven:**
    - Preheat your oven to 375°F (190°C).
9. **Bake:**
    - Bake in the preheated oven for 30-35 minutes, or until the loaf is golden brown and sounds hollow when tapped on the bottom.
10. **Cool:**
    - Remove the bread from the oven and let it cool in the pan for 10 minutes before transferring it to a wire rack to cool completely.

Enjoy your homemade Dreikornbrot! This flavorful three-grain bread is perfect for sandwiches, toasts, or simply enjoyed with butter or your favorite spread.

Helles Bauernbrot (Light Farmer's Bread)

Ingredients:

- **For the Dough:**
    - 3 ½ cups (440 g) all-purpose flour
    - 1 cup (120 g) whole wheat flour
    - 1 ¼ cups (300 ml) warm water (110°F or 45°C)
    - 2 teaspoons (6 g) active dry yeast
    - 1 tablespoon (15 g) sugar or honey
    - 2 teaspoons (10 g) salt
    - 2 tablespoons (30 ml) olive oil or melted butter

Instructions:

1. **Prepare the Yeast:**
    - In a small bowl, dissolve the sugar or honey in the warm water. Sprinkle the yeast over the surface and let it sit for 5-10 minutes, or until it becomes frothy and bubbly.
2. **Mix the Dough:**
    - In a large mixing bowl, combine the all-purpose flour, whole wheat flour, and salt.
    - Make a well in the center and add the yeast mixture and olive oil or melted butter.
    - Stir until a rough dough forms.
3. **Knead the Dough:**
    - Turn the dough out onto a lightly floured surface and knead for about 8-10 minutes, or until it becomes smooth and elastic. Alternatively, use a stand mixer with a dough hook for about 5 minutes.
4. **First Rise:**
    - Place the dough in a lightly greased bowl and cover it with plastic wrap or a damp cloth.
    - Let it rise in a warm place for about 1-1.5 hours, or until it has doubled in size.
5. **Shape the Dough:**
    - Punch down the risen dough to release air. Turn it out onto a lightly floured surface and shape it into a round or oval loaf.
    - Place the shaped dough onto a parchment-lined baking sheet or into a greased 9x5 inch (23x13 cm) loaf pan.
6. **Second Rise:**
    - Cover the loaf with plastic wrap or a damp cloth and let it rise for another 30-45 minutes, or until it has risen just above the edge of the pan or is puffy.
7. **Preheat Oven:**
    - Preheat your oven to 375°F (190°C).
8. **Bake:**
    - Bake in the preheated oven for 30-35 minutes, or until the loaf is golden brown and sounds hollow when tapped on the bottom.
9. **Cool:**
    - Remove the bread from the oven and let it cool in the pan for 10 minutes before transferring it to a wire rack to cool completely.

Enjoy your homemade Helles Bauernbrot! This light farmer's bread has a soft, airy texture and is perfect for sandwiches, toast, or enjoyed with a bit of butter and jam.

Dinkel-Sauerteigbrot (Spelt Sourdough Bread)

Ingredients:

- **For the Sourdough Starter:**
    - ¼ cup (60 g) active spelt sourdough starter (fed and bubbly)
    - ½ cup (120 ml) warm water (110°F or 45°C)
    - ½ cup (60 g) spelt flour
- **For the Dough:**
    - 1 ¼ cups (300 ml) warm water (110°F or 45°C)
    - 3 cups (360 g) spelt flour
    - 1 teaspoon (5 g) salt
    - 1 tablespoon (15 g) honey or maple syrup (optional, for a slightly sweeter dough)
    - 1 cup (240 g) active spelt sourdough starter (prepared from the above)

Instructions:

1. **Prepare the Sourdough Starter:**
    - In a small bowl, mix the spelt flour, warm water, and active sourdough starter.
    - Cover and let it sit at room temperature for 8-12 hours, or until it is bubbly and has a pleasant tangy smell.
2. **Mix the Dough:**
    - In a large mixing bowl, combine the spelt flour and salt.
    - Make a well in the center and add the prepared sourdough starter, warm water, and honey or maple syrup if using.
    - Stir until a rough dough forms.
3. **Knead the Dough:**
    - Turn the dough out onto a lightly floured surface and knead for about 8-10 minutes, or until it becomes smooth and elastic. Alternatively, use a stand mixer with a dough hook for about 5 minutes.
4. **First Rise:**
    - Place the dough in a lightly greased bowl and cover it with plastic wrap or a damp cloth.
    - Let it rise in a warm place for about 4-6 hours, or until it has doubled in size. This time can vary based on the strength of your starter and ambient temperature.
5. **Shape the Bread:**
    - Punch down the risen dough to release air. Turn it out onto a lightly floured surface and shape it into a loaf.
    - Place the shaped dough into a greased 9x5 inch (23x13 cm) loaf pan or onto a parchment-lined baking sheet if making a free-form loaf.
6. **Second Rise:**
    - Cover the loaf with plastic wrap or a damp cloth and let it rise for another 1-2 hours, or until it has risen just above the edge of the pan or is puffy.

7. **Preheat Oven:**
   - Preheat your oven to 375°F (190°C).
8. **Bake:**
   - For a crustier loaf, you can make a few shallow slashes on the top of the dough with a sharp knife or bread lame.
   - Bake in the preheated oven for 30-35 minutes, or until the loaf is golden brown and sounds hollow when tapped on the bottom.
9. **Cool:**
   - Remove the bread from the oven and let it cool in the pan for 10 minutes before transferring it to a wire rack to cool completely.

Enjoy your homemade Dinkel-Sauerteigbrot! The spelt flour gives this sourdough bread a lovely nutty flavor and a hearty texture, making it perfect for sandwiches, toast, or just enjoying with a bit of butter.

Roggenvollkornbrot (Rye Whole Grain Bread)

Ingredients:

- **For the Dough:**
    - 3 cups (360 g) whole rye flour
    - 1 ¼ cups (300 ml) warm water (110°F or 45°C)
    - 2 teaspoons (6 g) active dry yeast
    - 1 tablespoon (15 g) honey or molasses
    - 2 teaspoons (10 g) salt
    - 1 tablespoon (15 ml) vegetable oil or melted butter
- **For the Soaker (optional but recommended for better texture):**
    - ¼ cup (30 g) whole rye flour
    - ¼ cup (30 g) rolled oats or cracked rye
    - ½ cup (120 ml) warm water

Instructions:

1. **Prepare the Soaker (if using):**
    - In a small bowl, combine the whole rye flour, rolled oats or cracked rye, and warm water.
    - Mix well and let it sit at room temperature for at least 1 hour, or overnight if you prefer.
2. **Prepare the Yeast:**
    - In a small bowl, dissolve the honey or molasses in the warm water. Sprinkle the yeast over the surface and let it sit for 5-10 minutes, or until it becomes frothy and bubbly.
3. **Mix the Dough:**
    - In a large mixing bowl, combine the whole rye flour and salt.
    - Make a well in the center and add the yeast mixture, vegetable oil or melted butter, and the prepared soaker (if using).
    - Stir until a rough, shaggy dough forms. Rye doughs are typically very sticky and dense.
4. **Knead the Dough:**
    - Transfer the dough to a lightly floured surface and knead for about 5 minutes. Rye dough is denser and stickier than wheat dough, so it may not become as smooth. Alternatively, use a stand mixer with a dough hook, mixing for about 5 minutes.
5. **First Rise:**
    - Place the dough in a lightly greased bowl and cover it with plastic wrap or a damp cloth.
    - Let it rise in a warm place for about 1-1.5 hours, or until it has risen slightly. Rye bread doesn't rise as much as wheat bread, so it may not double in size.

6. **Shape the Bread:**
    - Punch down the risen dough to release air. Turn it out onto a lightly floured surface and shape it into a loaf.
    - Place the shaped dough into a greased 9x5 inch (23x13 cm) loaf pan or onto a parchment-lined baking sheet if making a free-form loaf.
7. **Second Rise:**
    - Cover the loaf with plastic wrap or a damp cloth and let it rise for another 30-45 minutes, or until it has risen slightly above the edge of the pan or is puffy.
8. **Preheat Oven:**
    - Preheat your oven to 375°F (190°C).
9. **Bake:**
    - Bake in the preheated oven for 35-45 minutes, or until the loaf is dark brown and sounds hollow when tapped on the bottom.
10. **Cool:**
    - Remove the bread from the oven and let it cool in the pan for 10 minutes before transferring it to a wire rack to cool completely.

Enjoy your homemade Roggenvollkornbrot! This rye whole grain bread is perfect for hearty sandwiches, or simply enjoyed with a bit of butter or cheese.

Pizzabrot (Pizza Bread)

Ingredients:

- **For the Dough:**
    - 3 ½ cups (440 g) all-purpose flour
    - 1 cup (240 ml) warm water (110°F or 45°C)
    - 2 teaspoons (6 g) active dry yeast
    - 1 tablespoon (15 g) sugar
    - 1 teaspoon (5 g) salt
    - 2 tablespoons (30 ml) olive oil
- **For the Topping:**
    - 1 cup (100 g) shredded mozzarella cheese
    - ¼ cup (30 g) grated Parmesan cheese
    - ½ cup (75 g) pizza sauce or marinara sauce
    - 1 teaspoon dried oregano
    - 1 teaspoon dried basil
    - 1 teaspoon garlic powder
    - Optional: sliced olives, pepperoni, or other favorite pizza toppings

Instructions:

1. **Prepare the Yeast:**
    - In a small bowl, dissolve the sugar in the warm water. Sprinkle the yeast over the surface and let it sit for 5-10 minutes, or until it becomes frothy and bubbly.
2. **Mix the Dough:**
    - In a large mixing bowl, combine the flour and salt.
    - Make a well in the center and add the yeast mixture and olive oil.
    - Stir until a rough dough forms.
3. **Knead the Dough:**
    - Turn the dough out onto a lightly floured surface and knead for about 8-10 minutes, or until it becomes smooth and elastic. Alternatively, use a stand mixer with a dough hook for about 5 minutes.
4. **First Rise:**
    - Place the dough in a lightly greased bowl and cover it with plastic wrap or a damp cloth.
    - Let it rise in a warm place for about 1-1.5 hours, or until it has doubled in size.
5. **Prepare the Topping:**
    - In a small bowl, mix together the oregano, basil, and garlic powder. Set aside.
6. **Shape the Dough:**
    - Punch down the risen dough to release air. Turn it out onto a lightly floured surface and shape it into a rectangular or round loaf, depending on your preference.

- Place the shaped dough onto a parchment-lined baking sheet or into a greased 9x13 inch (23x33 cm) baking pan.
7. **Second Rise:**
   - Cover the loaf with plastic wrap or a damp cloth and let it rise for another 30-45 minutes, or until it has risen slightly.
8. **Preheat Oven:**
   - Preheat your oven to 375°F (190°C).
9. **Add the Toppings:**
   - Spread the pizza sauce or marinara sauce over the top of the dough, leaving a small border around the edges.
   - Sprinkle the shredded mozzarella and grated Parmesan cheese evenly over the sauce.
   - Add any additional toppings like sliced olives or pepperoni if desired.
   - Sprinkle the oregano, basil, and garlic powder mixture over the cheese.
10. **Bake:**
    - Bake in the preheated oven for 20-25 minutes, or until the bread is golden brown and the cheese is bubbly and slightly browned.
11. **Cool:**
    - Remove the bread from the oven and let it cool for a few minutes before slicing.

Enjoy your homemade Pizzabrot! This pizza-flavored bread is perfect for serving alongside soups and salads, or for enjoying on its own.

Roggen-Kartoffelbrot (Rye Potato Bread)

Ingredients:

- **For the Dough:**
    - 2 cups (240 g) whole rye flour
    - 1 cup (120 g) all-purpose flour
    - 1 ½ cups (360 ml) warm water (110°F or 45°C)
    - 1 cup (200 g) mashed potatoes (cooled, from about 2 medium potatoes)
    - 2 teaspoons (6 g) active dry yeast
    - 1 tablespoon (15 g) honey or molasses
    - 2 teaspoons (10 g) salt
    - 2 tablespoons (30 ml) vegetable oil or melted butter
- **For the Potato Mash:**
    - 2 medium potatoes
    - Salt and pepper to taste

Instructions:

1. **Prepare the Potato Mash:**
    - Peel and cut the potatoes into chunks. Boil them in salted water until tender, about 15-20 minutes.
    - Drain the potatoes and mash them until smooth. Let them cool to room temperature before using.
2. **Prepare the Yeast:**
    - In a small bowl, dissolve the honey or molasses in the warm water. Sprinkle the yeast over the surface and let it sit for 5-10 minutes, or until it becomes frothy and bubbly.
3. **Mix the Dough:**
    - In a large mixing bowl, combine the rye flour and all-purpose flour.
    - Make a well in the center and add the yeast mixture, mashed potatoes, and vegetable oil or melted butter.
    - Stir until a rough dough forms.
4. **Knead the Dough:**
    - Turn the dough out onto a lightly floured surface and knead for about 8-10 minutes, or until it becomes smooth and elastic. Rye dough will be stickier and denser compared to wheat dough. Alternatively, use a stand mixer with a dough hook for about 5 minutes.
5. **First Rise:**
    - Place the dough in a lightly greased bowl and cover it with plastic wrap or a damp cloth.
    - Let it rise in a warm place for about 1-1.5 hours, or until it has doubled in size.
6. **Shape the Bread:**

- Punch down the risen dough to release air. Turn it out onto a lightly floured surface and shape it into a loaf.
- Place the shaped dough into a greased 9x5 inch (23x13 cm) loaf pan or onto a parchment-lined baking sheet if making a free-form loaf.

7. **Second Rise:**
   - Cover the loaf with plastic wrap or a damp cloth and let it rise for another 30-45 minutes, or until it has risen just above the edge of the pan or is puffy.
8. **Preheat Oven:**
   - Preheat your oven to 375°F (190°C).
9. **Bake:**
   - Bake in the preheated oven for 35-45 minutes, or until the loaf is deep golden brown and sounds hollow when tapped on the bottom.
10. **Cool:**
    - Remove the bread from the oven and let it cool in the pan for 10 minutes before transferring it to a wire rack to cool completely.

Enjoy your homemade Roggen-Kartoffelbrot! This rye potato bread is perfect for sandwiches, served with soups, or enjoyed with a bit of butter. Its moist, dense crumb and rich flavor make it a hearty and satisfying choice.

Kornspitz (Grain Spitz)

Ingredients:

- **For the Dough:**
    - 2 cups (240 g) whole rye flour
    - 1 cup (120 g) all-purpose flour
    - 1 ½ cups (360 ml) warm water (110°F or 45°C)
    - 1 cup (200 g) mashed potatoes (cooled, from about 2 medium potatoes)
    - 2 teaspoons (6 g) active dry yeast
    - 1 tablespoon (15 g) honey or molasses
    - 2 teaspoons (10 g) salt
    - 2 tablespoons (30 ml) vegetable oil or melted butter
- **For the Potato Mash:**
    - 2 medium potatoes
    - Salt and pepper to taste

Instructions:

1. **Prepare the Potato Mash:**
   - Peel and cut the potatoes into chunks. Boil them in salted water until tender, about 15-20 minutes.
   - Drain the potatoes and mash them until smooth. Let them cool to room temperature before using.
2. **Prepare the Yeast:**
   - In a small bowl, dissolve the honey or molasses in the warm water. Sprinkle the yeast over the surface and let it sit for 5-10 minutes, or until it becomes frothy and bubbly.
3. **Mix the Dough:**
   - In a large mixing bowl, combine the rye flour and all-purpose flour.
   - Make a well in the center and add the yeast mixture, mashed potatoes, and vegetable oil or melted butter.
   - Stir until a rough dough forms.
4. **Knead the Dough:**
   - Turn the dough out onto a lightly floured surface and knead for about 8-10 minutes, or until it becomes smooth and elastic. Rye dough will be stickier and denser compared to wheat dough. Alternatively, use a stand mixer with a dough hook for about 5 minutes.
5. **First Rise:**
   - Place the dough in a lightly greased bowl and cover it with plastic wrap or a damp cloth.
   - Let it rise in a warm place for about 1-1.5 hours, or until it has doubled in size.
6. **Shape the Bread:**

- Punch down the risen dough to release air. Turn it out onto a lightly floured surface and shape it into a loaf.
- Place the shaped dough into a greased 9x5 inch (23x13 cm) loaf pan or onto a parchment-lined baking sheet if making a free-form loaf.

7. **Second Rise:**
   - Cover the loaf with plastic wrap or a damp cloth and let it rise for another 30-45 minutes, or until it has risen just above the edge of the pan or is puffy.
8. **Preheat Oven:**
   - Preheat your oven to 375°F (190°C).
9. **Bake:**
   - Bake in the preheated oven for 35-45 minutes, or until the loaf is deep golden brown and sounds hollow when tapped on the bottom.
10. **Cool:**
    - Remove the bread from the oven and let it cool in the pan for 10 minutes before transferring it to a wire rack to cool completely.

Enjoy your homemade Roggen-Kartoffelbrot! This rye potato bread is perfect for sandwiches, served with soups, or enjoyed with a bit of butter. Its moist, dense crumb and rich flavor make it a hearty and satisfying choice.

Kornspitz (Grain Spitz)

Ingredients:

- **For the Dough:**
    - 3 ½ cups (440 g) all-purpose flour
    - 1 cup (120 g) whole wheat flour
    - 1 cup (120 g) mixed grains (such as rolled oats, sunflower seeds, flaxseeds, and pumpkin seeds)
    - 1 ¼ cups (300 ml) warm water (110°F or 45°C)
    - 2 teaspoons (6 g) active dry yeast
    - 1 tablespoon (15 g) honey or sugar
    - 1 teaspoon (5 g) salt
    - 2 tablespoons (30 ml) olive oil or vegetable oil
- **For the Topping:**
    - ¼ cup (30 g) mixed seeds (such as sunflower seeds, sesame seeds, and poppy seeds)
    - 1 egg (for egg wash)

Instructions:

1. **Prepare the Yeast:**
    - In a small bowl, dissolve the honey or sugar in the warm water. Sprinkle the yeast over the surface and let it sit for 5-10 minutes, or until it becomes frothy and bubbly.
2. **Mix the Dough:**
    - In a large mixing bowl, combine the all-purpose flour, whole wheat flour, and salt.
    - Make a well in the center and add the yeast mixture and olive oil.
    - Stir until a rough dough forms. Then, fold in the mixed grains.
3. **Knead the Dough:**
    - Turn the dough out onto a lightly floured surface and knead for about 8-10 minutes, or until it becomes smooth and elastic. Alternatively, use a stand mixer with a dough hook for about 5 minutes.
4. **First Rise:**
    - Place the dough in a lightly greased bowl and cover it with plastic wrap or a damp cloth.
    - Let it rise in a warm place for about 1-1.5 hours, or until it has doubled in size.
5. **Shape the Rolls:**
    - Punch down the risen dough to release air. Turn it out onto a lightly floured surface and divide it into 12-16 equal pieces.
    - Shape each piece into a pointed roll (spitz shape) by rolling and tapering the ends. Alternatively, shape into small rounded rolls if you prefer.
6. **Prepare for Baking:**

- Place the shaped rolls onto a parchment-lined baking sheet or a greased baking sheet.
- Brush each roll with the beaten egg for a glossy finish and sprinkle with mixed seeds.

7. **Second Rise:**
   - Cover the rolls with plastic wrap or a damp cloth and let them rise for another 30-45 minutes, or until they have puffed up and almost doubled in size.
8. **Preheat Oven:**
   - Preheat your oven to 425°F (220°C).
9. **Bake:**
   - Bake in the preheated oven for 20-25 minutes, or until the rolls are golden brown and sound hollow when tapped on the bottom.
10. **Cool:**
    - Remove the rolls from the oven and let them cool on a wire rack.

Enjoy your homemade Kornspitz! These grain rolls are perfect for breakfast, as a sandwich roll, or alongside soups and salads. Their crunchy exterior and nutty interior make them a delightful addition to any meal.

Kümmelbrot (Caraway Bread)

Ingredients:

- **For the Dough:**
    - 3 cups (360 g) all-purpose flour
    - 1 cup (120 g) whole wheat flour
    - 1 ¼ cups (300 ml) warm water (110°F or 45°C)
    - 2 teaspoons (6 g) active dry yeast
    - 1 tablespoon (15 g) sugar or honey
    - 2 teaspoons (10 g) salt
    - 2 tablespoons (30 ml) vegetable oil or melted butter
    - 2 tablespoons (15 g) caraway seeds
- **For the Topping:**
    - 1 tablespoon (10 g) caraway seeds
    - 1 egg (for egg wash, optional)

Instructions:

1. **Prepare the Yeast:**
    - In a small bowl, dissolve the sugar or honey in the warm water. Sprinkle the yeast over the surface and let it sit for 5-10 minutes, or until it becomes frothy and bubbly.
2. **Mix the Dough:**
    - In a large mixing bowl, combine the all-purpose flour, whole wheat flour, and salt.
    - Make a well in the center and add the yeast mixture, vegetable oil or melted butter, and caraway seeds.
    - Stir until a rough dough forms.
3. **Knead the Dough:**
    - Turn the dough out onto a lightly floured surface and knead for about 8-10 minutes, or until it becomes smooth and elastic. Alternatively, use a stand mixer with a dough hook for about 5 minutes.
4. **First Rise:**
    - Place the dough in a lightly greased bowl and cover it with plastic wrap or a damp cloth.
    - Let it rise in a warm place for about 1-1.5 hours, or until it has doubled in size.
5. **Shape the Bread:**
    - Punch down the risen dough to release air. Turn it out onto a lightly floured surface and shape it into a loaf or divide it into smaller rolls if desired.
    - Place the shaped dough onto a parchment-lined baking sheet or into a greased 9x5 inch (23x13 cm) loaf pan.
6. **Prepare for Baking:**
    - Brush the top of the dough with a beaten egg if you prefer a glossy finish.

- Sprinkle the additional caraway seeds over the top.
7. **Second Rise:**
    - Cover the loaf or rolls with plastic wrap or a damp cloth and let them rise for another 30-45 minutes, or until they have puffed up and almost doubled in size.
8. **Preheat Oven:**
    - Preheat your oven to 375°F (190°C).
9. **Bake:**
    - Bake in the preheated oven for 30-35 minutes, or until the loaf or rolls are golden brown and sound hollow when tapped on the bottom.
10. **Cool:**
    - Remove the bread from the oven and let it cool in the pan for 10 minutes before transferring it to a wire rack to cool completely.

Enjoy your homemade Kümmelbrot! The caraway seeds impart a lovely, aromatic flavor to this bread, making it an excellent choice for sandwiches, served with hearty soups, or enjoyed with a simple spread of butter.

Kümmelbrot (Caraway Bread)

Ingredients:

- **For the Dough:**
    - 3 cups (360 g) all-purpose flour
    - 1 cup (120 g) whole wheat flour
    - 1 ¼ cups (300 ml) warm water (110°F or 45°C)
    - 2 teaspoons (6 g) active dry yeast
    - 1 tablespoon (15 g) sugar or honey
    - 2 teaspoons (10 g) salt
    - 2 tablespoons (30 ml) vegetable oil or melted butter
    - 2 tablespoons (15 g) caraway seeds
- **For the Topping:**
    - 1 tablespoon (10 g) caraway seeds
    - 1 egg (for egg wash, optional)

Instructions:

1. **Prepare the Yeast:**
    - In a small bowl, dissolve the sugar or honey in the warm water. Sprinkle the yeast over the surface and let it sit for 5-10 minutes, or until it becomes frothy and bubbly.
2. **Mix the Dough:**
    - In a large mixing bowl, combine the all-purpose flour, whole wheat flour, and salt.
    - Make a well in the center and add the yeast mixture, vegetable oil or melted butter, and caraway seeds.
    - Stir until a rough dough forms.
3. **Knead the Dough:**
    - Turn the dough out onto a lightly floured surface and knead for about 8-10 minutes, or until it becomes smooth and elastic. Alternatively, use a stand mixer with a dough hook for about 5 minutes.
4. **First Rise:**
    - Place the dough in a lightly greased bowl and cover it with plastic wrap or a damp cloth.
    - Let it rise in a warm place for about 1-1.5 hours, or until it has doubled in size.
5. **Shape the Bread:**
    - Punch down the risen dough to release air. Turn it out onto a lightly floured surface and shape it into a loaf or divide it into smaller rolls if desired.
    - Place the shaped dough onto a parchment-lined baking sheet or into a greased 9x5 inch (23x13 cm) loaf pan.
6. **Prepare for Baking:**
    - Brush the top of the dough with a beaten egg if you prefer a glossy finish.

- Sprinkle the additional caraway seeds over the top.
7. **Second Rise:**
   - Cover the loaf or rolls with plastic wrap or a damp cloth and let them rise for another 30-45 minutes, or until they have puffed up and almost doubled in size.
8. **Preheat Oven:**
   - Preheat your oven to 375°F (190°C).
9. **Bake:**
   - Bake in the preheated oven for 30-35 minutes, or until the loaf or rolls are golden brown and sound hollow when tapped on the bottom.
10. **Cool:**
    - Remove the bread from the oven and let it cool in the pan for 10 minutes before transferring it to a wire rack to cool completely.

Enjoy your homemade Kümmelbrot! This bread's caraway seeds add a unique and aromatic flavor, making it a great choice for hearty meals or a satisfying snack.

Franzbrötchen (Cinnamon Croissants)

Ingredients:

- **For the Dough:**
    - 3 ½ cups (440 g) all-purpose flour
    - ¼ cup (50 g) sugar
    - 1 teaspoon (5 g) salt
    - 1 tablespoon (10 g) active dry yeast
    - 1 cup (240 ml) warm milk (110°F or 45°C)
    - ½ cup (115 g) unsalted butter, softened
    - 2 large eggs
- **For the Filling:**
    - ½ cup (115 g) unsalted butter, softened
    - ¾ cup (150 g) brown sugar
    - 2 tablespoons (15 g) ground cinnamon
- **For the Glaze:**
    - 1 egg (for egg wash)
    - 1 tablespoon (15 ml) milk (for egg wash)

Instructions:

1. **Prepare the Dough:**
    - In a small bowl, dissolve the sugar in the warm milk and sprinkle the yeast over the surface. Let it sit for 5-10 minutes, or until it becomes frothy.
    - In a large mixing bowl, combine the flour and salt.
    - Make a well in the center and add the yeast mixture, softened butter, and eggs.
    - Mix until a dough forms. Knead on a floured surface for about 8-10 minutes, or until the dough is smooth and elastic. Alternatively, use a stand mixer with a dough hook for about 5 minutes.
2. **First Rise:**
    - Place the dough in a lightly greased bowl and cover it with plastic wrap or a damp cloth.
    - Let it rise in a warm place for about 1-1.5 hours, or until it has doubled in size.
3. **Prepare the Filling:**
    - In a medium bowl, mix together the softened butter, brown sugar, and ground cinnamon until well combined.
4. **Roll and Shape the Dough:**
    - Punch down the risen dough and turn it out onto a lightly floured surface.
    - Roll the dough into a large rectangle, approximately 12x16 inches (30x40 cm).
    - Spread the cinnamon filling evenly over the dough, leaving a small border around the edges.
    - Roll the dough tightly from one long side to the other to form a log.

- Using a sharp knife, cut the log into 12-15 slices (about 1 inch or 2.5 cm thick).
5. **Shape the Pastries:**
   - Place the slices onto a parchment-lined baking sheet, spacing them a little apart.
   - Gently press down the center of each slice with your fingers or the handle of a wooden spoon to create the characteristic Franzbrötchen shape.
   - Use a sharp knife to make a few diagonal slashes on each pastry.
6. **Second Rise:**
   - Cover the pastries with plastic wrap or a damp cloth and let them rise for about 30 minutes.
7. **Preheat Oven:**
   - Preheat your oven to 375°F (190°C).
8. **Glaze and Bake:**
   - In a small bowl, mix the egg with the milk to create the egg wash. Brush the egg wash over the top of each pastry.
   - Bake in the preheated oven for 15-20 minutes, or until the pastries are golden brown and cooked through.
9. **Cool:**
   - Remove the Franzbrötchen from the oven and let them cool on a wire rack.

Enjoy your homemade Franzbrötchen! These cinnamon croissants are perfect for breakfast or as a sweet treat with a cup of coffee or tea. Their flaky texture and sweet cinnamon filling make them a delightful addition to any pastry lineup.

Brot mit Walnüssen (Walnut Bread)

Ingredients:

- **For the Dough:**
    - 3 cups (360 g) all-purpose flour
    - 1 cup (120 g) whole wheat flour
    - 1 ¼ cups (300 ml) warm water (110°F or 45°C)
    - 2 teaspoons (6 g) active dry yeast
    - 1 tablespoon (15 g) sugar or honey
    - 1 teaspoon (5 g) salt
    - 2 tablespoons (30 ml) olive oil or vegetable oil
    - 1 cup (120 g) walnuts, chopped

Instructions:

1. **Prepare the Yeast:**
    - In a small bowl, dissolve the sugar or honey in the warm water. Sprinkle the yeast over the surface and let it sit for 5-10 minutes, or until it becomes frothy and bubbly.
2. **Mix the Dough:**
    - In a large mixing bowl, combine the all-purpose flour, whole wheat flour, and salt.
    - Make a well in the center and add the yeast mixture and olive oil.
    - Stir until a rough dough forms.
3. **Knead the Dough:**
    - Turn the dough out onto a lightly floured surface and knead for about 8-10 minutes, or until it becomes smooth and elastic. Alternatively, use a stand mixer with a dough hook for about 5 minutes.
    - Add the chopped walnuts during the last few minutes of kneading, ensuring they are evenly distributed throughout the dough.
4. **First Rise:**
    - Place the dough in a lightly greased bowl and cover it with plastic wrap or a damp cloth.
    - Let it rise in a warm place for about 1-1.5 hours, or until it has doubled in size.
5. **Shape the Bread:**
    - Punch down the risen dough to release air. Turn it out onto a lightly floured surface and shape it into a loaf.
    - Place the shaped dough into a greased 9x5 inch (23x13 cm) loaf pan or onto a parchment-lined baking sheet if making a free-form loaf.
6. **Second Rise:**
    - Cover the loaf with plastic wrap or a damp cloth and let it rise for another 30-45 minutes, or until it has risen just above the edge of the pan or is puffy.
7. **Preheat Oven:**

        - Preheat your oven to 375°F (190°C).
8. **Bake:**
        - Bake in the preheated oven for 30-35 minutes, or until the loaf is golden brown and sounds hollow when tapped on the bottom.
9. **Cool:**
        - Remove the bread from the oven and let it cool in the pan for 10 minutes before transferring it to a wire rack to cool completely.

Enjoy your Brot mit Walnüssen! This walnut bread is delicious on its own or with a variety of spreads. Its nutty flavor and hearty texture make it a great addition to any meal.

Knoblauchbrot (Garlic Bread)

Ingredients:

- **For the Garlic Butter Spread:**
    - ½ cup (115 g) unsalted butter, softened
    - 4-5 cloves garlic, minced or grated
    - 2 tablespoons (2 g) fresh parsley, finely chopped (or 1 tablespoon dried parsley)
    - ¼ teaspoon (1 g) salt
    - ¼ teaspoon (1 g) black pepper
    - Optional: ¼ teaspoon (1 g) dried oregano or basil for extra flavor
- **For the Bread:**
    - 1 loaf of Italian bread, French bread, or ciabatta
    - Optional: ¼ cup (25 g) grated Parmesan cheese for extra flavor

Instructions:

1. **Prepare the Garlic Butter Spread:**
    - In a medium bowl, combine the softened butter, minced garlic, chopped parsley, salt, pepper, and optional dried oregano or basil.
    - Mix until well combined.
2. **Prepare the Bread:**
    - Preheat your oven to 375°F (190°C).
    - Slice the loaf of bread in half lengthwise. If you prefer smaller pieces, you can also slice it into individual pieces or segments at this point.
3. **Spread the Garlic Butter:**
    - Spread the garlic butter mixture evenly over the cut sides of the bread. Make sure to cover the entire surface for maximum flavor.
    - If using Parmesan cheese, sprinkle it evenly over the garlic butter.
4. **Bake:**
    - Place the bread halves (or individual pieces) on a baking sheet.
    - Bake in the preheated oven for 10-15 minutes, or until the edges are golden brown and the butter is melted and bubbly. For extra crispiness, you can broil the bread for an additional 1-2 minutes, but watch it closely to avoid burning.
5. **Serve:**
    - Remove the garlic bread from the oven and let it cool slightly before slicing into pieces if you haven't already.
    - Serve warm.

Enjoy your homemade Knoblauchbrot! This garlic bread is a simple yet irresistible addition to any meal, offering a delightful combination of buttery and garlicky flavors.

Kaisersemmel (Kaiser Rolls)

Ingredients:

- **For the Dough:**
    - 3 ½ cups (440 g) all-purpose flour
    - 1 cup (120 g) bread flour (optional, for extra crispness)
    - 1 ¼ cups (300 ml) warm water (110°F or 45°C)
    - 2 teaspoons (6 g) active dry yeast
    - 1 tablespoon (15 g) sugar
    - 1 teaspoon (5 g) salt
    - 2 tablespoons (30 ml) vegetable oil or melted butter
- **For the Topping:**
    - 1 tablespoon (15 ml) water (for steam)
    - 1 tablespoon (10 g) flour (for dusting, optional)
    - 1 egg (for egg wash, optional)

Instructions:

1. **Prepare the Yeast:**
    - In a small bowl, dissolve the sugar in the warm water. Sprinkle the yeast over the surface and let it sit for 5-10 minutes, or until it becomes frothy and bubbly.
2. **Mix the Dough:**
    - In a large mixing bowl, combine the all-purpose flour, bread flour (if using), and salt.
    - Make a well in the center and add the yeast mixture and vegetable oil or melted butter.
    - Stir until a rough dough forms.
3. **Knead the Dough:**
    - Turn the dough out onto a lightly floured surface and knead for about 8-10 minutes, or until it becomes smooth and elastic. Alternatively, use a stand mixer with a dough hook for about 5 minutes.
4. **First Rise:**
    - Place the dough in a lightly greased bowl and cover it with plastic wrap or a damp cloth.
    - Let it rise in a warm place for about 1-1.5 hours, or until it has doubled in size.
5. **Shape the Rolls:**
    - Punch down the risen dough to release air. Turn it out onto a lightly floured surface and divide it into 8-10 equal pieces.
    - Shape each piece into a ball and place them on a parchment-lined baking sheet or a greased baking sheet.
    - Use a sharp knife or a dough scraper to make a cross pattern or the traditional Kaiser roll pattern on the top of each roll.

6. **Second Rise:**
   - Cover the rolls with plastic wrap or a damp cloth and let them rise for another 30-45 minutes, or until they have puffed up and nearly doubled in size.
7. **Preheat Oven:**
   - Preheat your oven to 425°F (220°C).
8. **Prepare for Baking:**
   - If using, brush the rolls with a beaten egg for a shiny finish.
   - Alternatively, dust the tops with a little flour for a rustic look.
   - Place a small oven-safe dish of water in the oven to create steam, which helps develop a crispy crust.
9. **Bake:**
   - Bake in the preheated oven for 15-20 minutes, or until the rolls are golden brown and sound hollow when tapped on the bottom.
10. **Cool:**
    - Remove the rolls from the oven and let them cool on a wire rack.

Enjoy your homemade Kaisersemmel! These rolls are perfect for sandwiches, as a side with soups, or simply enjoyed with a pat of butter. Their crispy crust and soft, fluffy interior make them a beloved classic.

Focaccia mit Kräutern (Herb Focaccia)

Ingredients:

- **For the Dough:**
    - 3 ½ cups (440 g) all-purpose flour
    - 1 ¼ cups (300 ml) warm water (110°F or 45°C)
    - 2 teaspoons (6 g) active dry yeast
    - 1 tablespoon (15 g) sugar
    - 1 teaspoon (5 g) salt
    - ¼ cup (60 ml) olive oil, plus extra for drizzling
- **For the Herb Topping:**
    - 2-3 tablespoons fresh rosemary, finely chopped (or 1-2 tablespoons dried rosemary)
    - 1 tablespoon fresh thyme, finely chopped (or 1 tablespoon dried thyme)
    - 2-3 cloves garlic, minced (optional)
    - 1 tablespoon coarse sea salt
    - 2 tablespoons olive oil

Instructions:

1. **Prepare the Yeast:**
    - In a small bowl, dissolve the sugar in the warm water. Sprinkle the yeast over the surface and let it sit for 5-10 minutes, or until it becomes frothy and bubbly.
2. **Mix the Dough:**
    - In a large mixing bowl, combine the flour and salt.
    - Make a well in the center and add the yeast mixture and olive oil.
    - Stir until a rough dough forms.
3. **Knead the Dough:**
    - Turn the dough out onto a lightly floured surface and knead for about 8-10 minutes, or until it becomes smooth and elastic. Alternatively, use a stand mixer with a dough hook for about 5 minutes.
4. **First Rise:**
    - Place the dough in a lightly greased bowl and cover it with plastic wrap or a damp cloth.
    - Let it rise in a warm place for about 1-1.5 hours, or until it has doubled in size.
5. **Prepare the Pan:**
    - Preheat your oven to 425°F (220°C).
    - Grease a baking sheet or line it with parchment paper. You can also use a 9x13 inch (23x33 cm) baking pan for a thicker focaccia or a larger pan for a thinner one.
6. **Shape the Dough:**

- Punch down the risen dough to release air. Turn it out onto the prepared baking sheet.
- Use your fingers to stretch and press the dough out to fit the pan, creating dimples all over the surface.

7. **Add the Herb Topping:**
   - Drizzle the top of the dough with olive oil.
   - Sprinkle the chopped rosemary, thyme, and minced garlic (if using) evenly over the dough.
   - Sprinkle with coarse sea salt.
8. **Second Rise:**
   - Cover the dough with plastic wrap or a damp cloth and let it rise for another 30 minutes, or until it has puffed up slightly.
9. **Bake:**
   - Bake in the preheated oven for 20-25 minutes, or until the focaccia is golden brown and has a crispy crust.
10. **Cool:**
    - Remove the focaccia from the oven and let it cool slightly on a wire rack before slicing.

Enjoy your homemade Herb Focaccia! This bread is perfect for dipping in olive oil, serving with soups and salads, or simply enjoying as a savory treat.

Rosenbrot (Rose Bread)

Ingredients:

- **For the Dough:**
    - 3 ½ cups (440 g) all-purpose flour
    - ¼ cup (50 g) sugar
    - 1 teaspoon (5 g) salt
    - 2 teaspoons (6 g) active dry yeast
    - 1 cup (240 ml) warm milk (110°F or 45°C)
    - ¼ cup (60 g) unsalted butter, softened
    - 1 large egg
- **For the Filling:**
    - ½ cup (115 g) unsalted butter, softened
    - ¼ cup (50 g) sugar
    - 2 tablespoons (15 g) ground cinnamon
    - Optional: ¼ cup (30 g) finely chopped nuts or raisins
- **For the Glaze (optional):**
    - 1 egg, beaten
    - 1 tablespoon (15 ml) milk

Instructions:

1. **Prepare the Yeast:**
    - In a small bowl, dissolve the sugar in the warm milk. Sprinkle the yeast over the surface and let it sit for 5-10 minutes, or until it becomes frothy and bubbly.
2. **Mix the Dough:**
    - In a large mixing bowl, combine the flour and salt.
    - Make a well in the center and add the yeast mixture, softened butter, and egg.
    - Stir until a rough dough forms.
3. **Knead the Dough:**
    - Turn the dough out onto a lightly floured surface and knead for about 8-10 minutes, or until it becomes smooth and elastic. Alternatively, use a stand mixer with a dough hook for about 5 minutes.
4. **First Rise:**
    - Place the dough in a lightly greased bowl and cover it with plastic wrap or a damp cloth.
    - Let it rise in a warm place for about 1-1.5 hours, or until it has doubled in size.
5. **Prepare the Filling:**
    - In a small bowl, mix together the softened butter, sugar, and ground cinnamon until well combined. If using, stir in the chopped nuts or raisins.
6. **Shape the Bread:**

- Punch down the risen dough to release air. Turn it out onto a lightly floured surface.
- Roll the dough into a large rectangle, about 12x18 inches (30x45 cm).
- Spread the cinnamon filling evenly over the dough.
- Roll the dough tightly from one long side to the other to form a log.
- Slice the log into 12-15 even pieces.

7. **Form the Rose Shape:**
   - Place a slice of dough in the center of a greased or parchment-lined round baking pan.
   - Arrange the remaining slices around the center slice, slightly overlapping them to form a rose shape.
   - Gently press down the center of each piece to help them adhere and form a cohesive shape.
8. **Second Rise:**
   - Cover the pan with plastic wrap or a damp cloth and let it rise for another 30-45 minutes, or until the dough has puffed up.
9. **Preheat Oven:**
   - Preheat your oven to 350°F (175°C).
10. **Glaze and Bake:**
    - If using, brush the top of the dough with the beaten egg mixed with milk for a glossy finish.
    - Bake in the preheated oven for 25-30 minutes, or until the bread is golden brown and sounds hollow when tapped on the bottom.
11. **Cool:**
    - Remove the bread from the oven and let it cool in the pan for 10 minutes before transferring it to a wire rack to cool completely.

Enjoy your homemade Rosenbrot! This beautiful rose-shaped bread is perfect for special occasions and will surely impress your guests with its elegant appearance and delicious taste.

Spelt Rye Bread

Ingredients:

- **For the Dough:**
    - 1 ½ cups (180 g) spelt flour
    - 1 ½ cups (180 g) rye flour
    - 1 cup (240 ml) warm water (110°F or 45°C)
    - 1 tablespoon (15 g) sugar or honey
    - 2 teaspoons (6 g) active dry yeast
    - 1 teaspoon (5 g) salt
    - 2 tablespoons (30 ml) vegetable oil or melted butter
    - Optional: 1 tablespoon caraway seeds or fennel seeds for added flavor
- **For the Topping (optional):**
    - 1 tablespoon (10 g) caraway seeds or sunflower seeds

Instructions:

1. **Prepare the Yeast:**
    - In a small bowl, dissolve the sugar or honey in the warm water. Sprinkle the yeast over the surface and let it sit for 5-10 minutes, or until it becomes frothy and bubbly.
2. **Mix the Dough:**
    - In a large mixing bowl, combine the spelt flour, rye flour, and salt.
    - Make a well in the center and add the yeast mixture and vegetable oil or melted butter.
    - Stir until a rough dough forms. If using, fold in the caraway or fennel seeds.
3. **Knead the Dough:**
    - Turn the dough out onto a lightly floured surface and knead for about 8-10 minutes, or until it becomes smooth and elastic. The dough will be somewhat sticky due to the rye flour, but it should come together nicely. Alternatively, use a stand mixer with a dough hook for about 5 minutes.
4. **First Rise:**
    - Place the dough in a lightly greased bowl and cover it with plastic wrap or a damp cloth.
    - Let it rise in a warm place for about 1-1.5 hours, or until it has doubled in size.
5. **Shape the Bread:**
    - Punch down the risen dough to release air. Turn it out onto a lightly floured surface.
    - Shape the dough into a loaf. Place it in a greased 9x5 inch (23x13 cm) loaf pan or on a parchment-lined baking sheet if you prefer a free-form loaf.
6. **Second Rise:**

- Cover the loaf with plastic wrap or a damp cloth and let it rise for another 30-45 minutes, or until it has risen just above the edge of the pan or is puffy.

7. **Preheat Oven:**
   - Preheat your oven to 375°F (190°C).

8. **Prepare for Baking:**
   - If using, sprinkle the top of the loaf with caraway seeds or sunflower seeds.
   - Using a sharp knife, make a few slashes on top of the loaf to allow for expansion.

9. **Bake:**
   - Bake in the preheated oven for 30-35 minutes, or until the loaf is golden brown and sounds hollow when tapped on the bottom.

10. **Cool:**
    - Remove the bread from the oven and let it cool in the pan for 10 minutes before transferring it to a wire rack to cool completely.

Enjoy your Spelt Rye Bread! Its robust flavor and hearty texture make it a versatile and satisfying addition to your bread repertoire.

Karamell-Brot (Caramel Bread)

Ingredients:

- **For the Dough:**
    - 3 ½ cups (440 g) all-purpose flour
    - ¼ cup (50 g) sugar
    - 1 teaspoon (5 g) salt
    - 2 teaspoons (6 g) active dry yeast
    - 1 cup (240 ml) warm milk (110°F or 45°C)
    - ¼ cup (60 g) unsalted butter, softened
    - 1 large egg
- **For the Caramel Filling:**
    - ¼ cup (50 g) sugar
    - 2 tablespoons (30 g) unsalted butter
    - ¼ cup (60 ml) heavy cream
    - 1 teaspoon vanilla extract
- **For the Caramel Glaze (optional):**
    - ¼ cup (50 g) sugar
    - 2 tablespoons (30 g) unsalted butter
    - 2 tablespoons (30 ml) heavy cream

Instructions:

1. **Prepare the Caramel Filling:**
    - In a small saucepan over medium heat, combine the sugar and butter. Stir until melted and combined.
    - Slowly add the heavy cream, stirring continuously. Continue to cook for another 1-2 minutes until the mixture is smooth and slightly thickened.
    - Remove from heat and stir in the vanilla extract. Allow to cool slightly.
2. **Prepare the Dough:**
    - In a small bowl, dissolve the sugar in the warm milk. Sprinkle the yeast over the surface and let it sit for 5-10 minutes, or until it becomes frothy and bubbly.
    - In a large mixing bowl, combine the flour and salt.
    - Make a well in the center and add the yeast mixture, softened butter, and egg.
    - Stir until a rough dough forms.
3. **Knead the Dough:**
    - Turn the dough out onto a lightly floured surface and knead for about 8-10 minutes, or until it becomes smooth and elastic. Alternatively, use a stand mixer with a dough hook for about 5 minutes.
4. **First Rise:**
    - Place the dough in a lightly greased bowl and cover it with plastic wrap or a damp cloth.

- Let it rise in a warm place for about 1-1.5 hours, or until it has doubled in size.
5. **Shape the Bread:**
    - Punch down the risen dough to release air. Turn it out onto a lightly floured surface and roll it into a large rectangle, about 12x18 inches (30x45 cm).
    - Spread the slightly cooled caramel filling evenly over the dough.
    - Roll the dough tightly from one long side to the other to form a log.
    - Place the rolled dough in a greased 9x5 inch (23x13 cm) loaf pan or on a parchment-lined baking sheet if you prefer a free-form loaf.
6. **Second Rise:**
    - Cover the loaf with plastic wrap or a damp cloth and let it rise for another 30-45 minutes, or until it has risen just above the edge of the pan or is puffy.
7. **Preheat Oven:**
    - Preheat your oven to 375°F (190°C).
8. **Bake:**
    - Bake in the preheated oven for 30-35 minutes, or until the loaf is golden brown and sounds hollow when tapped on the bottom.
9. **Prepare the Caramel Glaze (optional):**
    - In a small saucepan over medium heat, combine the sugar and butter. Stir until melted and combined.
    - Slowly add the heavy cream, stirring continuously. Continue to cook for another 1-2 minutes until the mixture is smooth.
    - Remove from heat and allow to cool slightly.
10. **Cool and Glaze:**
    - Remove the bread from the oven and let it cool in the pan for 10 minutes before transferring it to a wire rack.
    - Brush the slightly cooled caramel glaze over the top of the bread if desired.

Enjoy your homemade Karamell-Brot! The combination of sweet caramel and soft bread makes this a delicious and special treat.

Mischbrot mit Kräutern (Herb Mixed Bread)

Ingredients:

- **For the Dough:**
    - 2 cups (250 g) all-purpose flour
    - 1 cup (120 g) whole wheat flour
    - 1 cup (120 g) rye flour
    - 1 ½ cups (360 ml) warm water (110°F or 45°C)
    - 2 teaspoons (6 g) active dry yeast
    - 1 tablespoon (15 g) sugar or honey
    - 1 ½ teaspoons (9 g) salt
    - 2 tablespoons (30 ml) olive oil or melted butter
- **For the Herb Mixture:**
    - 2 tablespoons fresh rosemary, finely chopped (or 1 tablespoon dried rosemary)
    - 2 tablespoons fresh thyme, finely chopped (or 1 tablespoon dried thyme)
    - 1 tablespoon fresh basil, finely chopped (or 1 tablespoon dried basil)
    - 2 cloves garlic, minced (optional)
    - 1 tablespoon mixed seeds (e.g., sunflower, pumpkin) for topping (optional)

Instructions:

1. **Prepare the Yeast:**
    - In a small bowl, dissolve the sugar or honey in the warm water. Sprinkle the yeast over the surface and let it sit for 5-10 minutes, or until it becomes frothy and bubbly.
2. **Mix the Dough:**
    - In a large mixing bowl, combine the all-purpose flour, whole wheat flour, rye flour, and salt.
    - Make a well in the center and add the yeast mixture and olive oil or melted butter.
    - Stir until a rough dough forms.
3. **Add the Herbs:**
    - Fold in the fresh or dried herbs and minced garlic (if using) until evenly distributed throughout the dough.
4. **Knead the Dough:**
    - Turn the dough out onto a lightly floured surface and knead for about 8-10 minutes, or until it becomes smooth and elastic. Alternatively, use a stand mixer with a dough hook for about 5 minutes.
5. **First Rise:**
    - Place the dough in a lightly greased bowl and cover it with plastic wrap or a damp cloth.
    - Let it rise in a warm place for about 1-1.5 hours, or until it has doubled in size.
6. **Shape the Bread:**

- Punch down the risen dough to release air. Turn it out onto a lightly floured surface.
- Shape the dough into a loaf or divide it into two smaller loaves. Place the shaped dough into greased or parchment-lined baking pans.

7. **Second Rise:**
   - Cover the loaf or loaves with plastic wrap or a damp cloth and let them rise for another 30-45 minutes, or until they have risen just above the edge of the pan or are puffy.
8. **Preheat Oven:**
   - Preheat your oven to 375°F (190°C).
9. **Prepare for Baking:**
   - If using, sprinkle the tops of the loaves with mixed seeds for added texture and flavor.
   - Use a sharp knife to make a few slashes on top of the loaf to allow for expansion.
10. **Bake:**
    - Bake in the preheated oven for 30-35 minutes, or until the bread is golden brown and sounds hollow when tapped on the bottom.
11. **Cool:**
    - Remove the bread from the oven and let it cool in the pans for 10 minutes before transferring it to a wire rack to cool completely.

Enjoy your homemade Mischbrot mit Kräutern! This herb-infused mixed bread offers a delightful combination of flavors and textures, perfect for a variety of meals or simply enjoyed with a bit of butter.

Bärlauchbrot (Wild Garlic Bread)

Ingredients:

- **For the Dough:**
    - 3 ½ cups (440 g) all-purpose flour
    - 1 cup (120 g) whole wheat flour
    - 1 cup (120 g) rye flour
    - 1 ½ cups (360 ml) warm water (110°F or 45°C)
    - 2 teaspoons (6 g) active dry yeast
    - 1 tablespoon (15 g) sugar or honey
    - 1 ½ teaspoons (9 g) salt
    - 2 tablespoons (30 ml) olive oil or melted butter
- **For the Wild Garlic Mixture:**
    - 1 cup (60 g) fresh wild garlic leaves, finely chopped (or ½ cup dried wild garlic)
    - 2 cloves garlic, minced (optional, for extra garlic flavor)
    - 2 tablespoons olive oil
    - 1 tablespoon lemon juice (optional, for brightness)

Instructions:

1. **Prepare the Yeast:**
    - In a small bowl, dissolve the sugar or honey in the warm water. Sprinkle the yeast over the surface and let it sit for 5-10 minutes, or until it becomes frothy and bubbly.
2. **Prepare the Wild Garlic Mixture:**
    - If using fresh wild garlic, wash and finely chop the leaves. If using dried wild garlic, rehydrate it according to package instructions or use it as-is.
    - In a small bowl, mix the chopped wild garlic (or dried garlic), minced garlic (if using), olive oil, and lemon juice (if using). Set aside.
3. **Mix the Dough:**
    - In a large mixing bowl, combine the all-purpose flour, whole wheat flour, rye flour, and salt.
    - Make a well in the center and add the yeast mixture and olive oil or melted butter.
    - Stir until a rough dough forms.
4. **Add the Wild Garlic Mixture:**
    - Fold the wild garlic mixture into the dough until evenly distributed.
5. **Knead the Dough:**
    - Turn the dough out onto a lightly floured surface and knead for about 8-10 minutes, or until it becomes smooth and elastic. Alternatively, use a stand mixer with a dough hook for about 5 minutes.
6. **First Rise:**

- Place the dough in a lightly greased bowl and cover it with plastic wrap or a damp cloth.
- Let it rise in a warm place for about 1-1.5 hours, or until it has doubled in size.

7. **Shape the Bread:**
    - Punch down the risen dough to release air. Turn it out onto a lightly floured surface.
    - Shape the dough into a loaf or divide it into smaller loaves or rolls. Place the shaped dough into greased or parchment-lined baking pans.
8. **Second Rise:**
    - Cover the loaf or loaves with plastic wrap or a damp cloth and let them rise for another 30-45 minutes, or until they have risen just above the edge of the pan or are puffy.
9. **Preheat Oven:**
    - Preheat your oven to 375°F (190°C).
10. **Prepare for Baking:**
    - Use a sharp knife to make a few slashes on top of the loaf to allow for expansion.
11. **Bake:**
    - Bake in the preheated oven for 30-35 minutes, or until the bread is golden brown and sounds hollow when tapped on the bottom.
12. **Cool:**
    - Remove the bread from the oven and let it cool in the pan for 10 minutes before transferring it to a wire rack to cool completely.

Enjoy your Bärlauchbrot! This bread's unique wild garlic flavor adds a fresh and vibrant touch to your breadbasket. It pairs wonderfully with cheese, salads, or just a bit of butter.

Süßes Zopfgebäck (Sweet Braided Bread)

Ingredients:

- **For the Dough:**
    - 4 cups (500 g) all-purpose flour
    - ½ cup (100 g) sugar
    - 1 teaspoon (5 g) salt
    - 2 teaspoons (6 g) active dry yeast
    - 1 cup (240 ml) warm milk (110°F or 45°C)
    - ¼ cup (60 g) unsalted butter, softened
    - 2 large eggs
- **For the Filling (Optional):**
    - ¼ cup (60 g) unsalted butter, softened
    - ¼ cup (50 g) sugar
    - 2 tablespoons (15 g) ground cinnamon
    - ½ cup (50 g) chopped nuts, raisins, or chocolate chips
- **For the Glaze:**
    - 1 egg, beaten
    - 1 tablespoon (15 ml) milk
    - 2 tablespoons (25 g) sugar (optional, for sprinkling)

Instructions:

1. **Prepare the Yeast:**
    - In a small bowl, dissolve the sugar in the warm milk. Sprinkle the yeast over the surface and let it sit for 5-10 minutes, or until it becomes frothy and bubbly.
2. **Mix the Dough:**
    - In a large mixing bowl, combine the flour and salt.
    - Make a well in the center and add the yeast mixture, softened butter, and eggs.
    - Stir until a rough dough forms.
3. **Knead the Dough:**
    - Turn the dough out onto a lightly floured surface and knead for about 8-10 minutes, or until it becomes smooth and elastic. Alternatively, use a stand mixer with a dough hook for about 5 minutes.
4. **First Rise:**
    - Place the dough in a lightly greased bowl and cover it with plastic wrap or a damp cloth.
    - Let it rise in a warm place for about 1-1.5 hours, or until it has doubled in size.
5. **Prepare the Filling (Optional):**
    - In a small bowl, mix together the softened butter, sugar, and ground cinnamon until well combined. If using, add nuts, raisins, or chocolate chips.
6. **Shape the Bread:**

- Punch down the risen dough to release air. Turn it out onto a lightly floured surface.
- Roll the dough into a large rectangle, about 12x18 inches (30x45 cm).
- Spread the filling evenly over the dough, leaving a small border around the edges.
- Roll the dough tightly from one long side to the other to form a log.
- Slice the log in half lengthwise, leaving one end uncut. Twist the two halves together to form a braid. Alternatively, shape the dough into a simple braid or knot if preferred.
- Place the braided dough onto a greased or parchment-lined baking sheet.

7. **Second Rise:**
   - Cover the braided dough with plastic wrap or a damp cloth and let it rise for another 30-45 minutes, or until it has puffed up.
8. **Preheat Oven:**
   - Preheat your oven to 375°F (190°C).
9. **Prepare for Baking:**
   - Brush the top of the dough with the beaten egg mixed with milk for a glossy finish.
   - If desired, sprinkle with additional sugar for extra sweetness.
10. **Bake:**
    - Bake in the preheated oven for 25-30 minutes, or until the bread is golden brown and sounds hollow when tapped on the bottom.
11. **Cool:**
    - Remove the bread from the oven and let it cool on a wire rack.

Enjoy your Süßes Zopfgebäck! This sweet braided bread is perfect for sharing with family and friends and makes a lovely addition to any meal. It can be served plain or with a dusting of powdered sugar, or even a drizzle of icing if you're feeling extra indulgent.

Nussbrot (Nut Bread)

Ingredients:

- **For the Dough:**
    - 3 ½ cups (440 g) all-purpose flour
    - 1 cup (120 g) whole wheat flour
    - 1 cup (120 g) rye flour
    - 1 ½ cups (360 ml) warm water (110°F or 45°C)
    - 2 teaspoons (6 g) active dry yeast
    - 1 tablespoon (15 g) sugar or honey
    - 1 ½ teaspoons (9 g) salt
    - 2 tablespoons (30 ml) olive oil or melted butter
- **For the Nuts:**
    - 1 cup (120 g) mixed nuts (such as walnuts, almonds, hazelnuts, pecans), roughly chopped
    - ¼ cup (30 g) sunflower seeds or pumpkin seeds (optional)

Instructions:

1. **Prepare the Yeast:**
    - In a small bowl, dissolve the sugar or honey in the warm water. Sprinkle the yeast over the surface and let it sit for 5-10 minutes, or until it becomes frothy and bubbly.
2. **Mix the Dough:**
    - In a large mixing bowl, combine the all-purpose flour, whole wheat flour, rye flour, and salt.
    - Make a well in the center and add the yeast mixture and olive oil or melted butter.
    - Stir until a rough dough forms.
3. **Add the Nuts:**
    - Fold the chopped nuts and seeds (if using) into the dough until evenly distributed.
4. **Knead the Dough:**
    - Turn the dough out onto a lightly floured surface and knead for about 8-10 minutes, or until it becomes smooth and elastic. Alternatively, use a stand mixer with a dough hook for about 5 minutes.
5. **First Rise:**
    - Place the dough in a lightly greased bowl and cover it with plastic wrap or a damp cloth.
    - Let it rise in a warm place for about 1-1.5 hours, or until it has doubled in size.
6. **Shape the Bread:**
    - Punch down the risen dough to release air. Turn it out onto a lightly floured surface.
    - Shape the dough into a loaf or divide it into smaller loaves or rolls.

- Place the shaped dough into greased or parchment-lined baking pans or onto a baking sheet.
7. **Second Rise:**
    - Cover the loaf or loaves with plastic wrap or a damp cloth and let them rise for another 30-45 minutes, or until they have risen just above the edge of the pan or are puffy.
8. **Preheat Oven:**
    - Preheat your oven to 375°F (190°C).
9. **Prepare for Baking:**
    - If desired, sprinkle the top of the loaf with additional seeds or chopped nuts for extra texture.
    - Use a sharp knife to make a few slashes on top of the loaf to allow for expansion.
10. **Bake:**
    - Bake in the preheated oven for 30-35 minutes, or until the bread is golden brown and sounds hollow when tapped on the bottom.
11. **Cool:**
    - Remove the bread from the oven and let it cool in the pan for 10 minutes before transferring it to a wire rack to cool completely.

Enjoy your Nussbrot! This nutty bread is perfect for a variety of meals and snacks, and its hearty texture makes it a satisfying choice.

Roggenbrot mit Honig (Rye Honey Bread)

Ingredients:

- **For the Dough:**
    - 2 cups (240 g) rye flour
    - 1 cup (120 g) all-purpose flour
    - 1 ½ cups (360 ml) warm water (110°F or 45°C)
    - ¼ cup (60 g) honey
    - 2 teaspoons (6 g) active dry yeast
    - 1 tablespoon (15 g) sugar
    - 1 ½ teaspoons (9 g) salt
    - 2 tablespoons (30 ml) vegetable oil or melted butter
- **For the Glaze (optional):**
    - 2 tablespoons (30 g) honey
    - 2 tablespoons (30 ml) warm water

Instructions:

1. **Prepare the Yeast:**
    - In a small bowl, dissolve the sugar in the warm water. Sprinkle the yeast over the surface and let it sit for 5-10 minutes, or until it becomes frothy and bubbly.
2. **Mix the Dough:**
    - In a large mixing bowl, combine the rye flour, all-purpose flour, and salt.
    - Make a well in the center and add the yeast mixture, honey, and vegetable oil or melted butter.
    - Stir until a rough dough forms.
3. **Knead the Dough:**
    - Turn the dough out onto a lightly floured surface and knead for about 8-10 minutes, or until it becomes smooth and elastic. The dough will be quite sticky due to the rye flour, so you may need to use a dough scraper or wet your hands.
4. **First Rise:**
    - Place the dough in a lightly greased bowl and cover it with plastic wrap or a damp cloth.
    - Let it rise in a warm place for about 1-1.5 hours, or until it has doubled in size.
5. **Shape the Bread:**
    - Punch down the risen dough to release air. Turn it out onto a lightly floured surface.
    - Shape the dough into a loaf and place it in a greased 9x5 inch (23x13 cm) loaf pan. Alternatively, you can shape it into a free-form loaf and place it on a parchment-lined baking sheet.
6. **Second Rise:**
    - Cover the loaf with plastic wrap or a damp cloth and let it rise for another 30-45 minutes, or until it has risen just above the edge of the pan or is puffy.
7. **Preheat Oven:**
    - Preheat your oven to 375°F (190°C).
8. **Prepare for Baking:**

- If desired, mix the honey with warm water and brush it over the top of the loaf for a glossy finish.
- Use a sharp knife or bread lame to make a few slashes on top of the loaf to allow for expansion.

9. **Bake:**
    - Bake in the preheated oven for 30-35 minutes, or until the bread is golden brown and sounds hollow when tapped on the bottom.
10. **Cool:**
    - Remove the bread from the oven and let it cool in the pan for 10 minutes before transferring it to a wire rack to cool completely.

Enjoy your Roggenbrot mit Honig! This bread's combination of rye and honey creates a deliciously unique flavor that pairs wonderfully with cheeses, meats, or simply a pat of butter.

Vollkorn-Sauerteigbrot (Whole Grain Sourdough Bread)

Ingredients:

- **For the Starter:**
    - ½ cup (120 g) whole grain flour (such as whole wheat or spelt)
    - ¼ cup (60 ml) water (room temperature)
    - 1 tablespoon (15 g) sourdough starter (active)
- **For the Dough:**
    - 2 cups (240 g) whole grain flour (such as whole wheat or spelt)
    - 1 cup (120 g) all-purpose flour
    - 1 ½ cups (360 ml) water (room temperature)
    - 1 ½ teaspoons (9 g) salt
    - 1 tablespoon (15 g) honey or molasses (optional, for a touch of sweetness)

Instructions:

1. **Prepare the Starter:**
    - In a small bowl, mix the whole grain flour and water with the sourdough starter. Cover with a cloth or plastic wrap and let it sit at room temperature for 8-12 hours, or until it becomes bubbly and has a pleasant sour aroma.
2. **Mix the Dough:**
    - In a large mixing bowl, combine the whole grain flour, all-purpose flour, and salt.
    - Make a well in the center and add the bubbly starter, water, and honey or molasses (if using).
    - Stir until the dough comes together. It will be quite thick and sticky.
3. **Knead the Dough:**
    - Turn the dough out onto a lightly floured surface and knead for about 8-10 minutes, or until it becomes smooth and elastic. The dough will be dense due to the whole grain flour, so kneading thoroughly helps develop the gluten.
4. **First Rise:**
    - Place the dough in a lightly greased bowl and cover it with plastic wrap or a damp cloth.
    - Let it rise at room temperature for about 4-6 hours, or until it has doubled in size. The timing may vary depending on the activity of your starter and the ambient temperature.
5. **Shape the Bread:**
    - Punch down the risen dough to release air. Turn it out onto a lightly floured surface.
    - Shape the dough into a round or oval loaf, or place it into a greased or parchment-lined loaf pan.
    - If desired, you can also shape it into a round and place it in a well-floured banneton or proofing basket.

6. **Second Rise:**
   - Cover the shaped loaf with plastic wrap or a damp cloth and let it rise for another 1-2 hours, or until it has risen noticeably.
7. **Preheat Oven:**
   - Preheat your oven to 450°F (230°C). If using a Dutch oven or baking stone, place it in the oven to preheat as well.
8. **Prepare for Baking:**
   - If using a banneton, gently turn the dough out onto a parchment-lined baking sheet or into a preheated Dutch oven.
   - Score the top of the loaf with a sharp knife or bread lame to allow for expansion.
9. **Bake:**
   - Bake the bread in the preheated oven for 35-45 minutes, or until the bread is deep golden brown and sounds hollow when tapped on the bottom.
   - If using a Dutch oven, cover the pot with a lid for the first 20 minutes, then remove the lid for the remaining time to allow the crust to develop.
10. **Cool:**
    - Remove the bread from the oven and let it cool on a wire rack before slicing.

Enjoy your Vollkorn-Sauerteigbrot! This whole grain sourdough bread is not only nutritious but also has a wonderful depth of flavor that pairs well with a variety of toppings or can be enjoyed on its own.

Schwarzbrot (Black Bread)

Ingredients:

- **For the Dough:**
    - 2 cups (240 g) rye flour
    - 1 cup (120 g) whole wheat flour
    - 1 cup (120 g) all-purpose flour
    - 1 ½ cups (360 ml) warm water (110°F or 45°C)
    - ¼ cup (60 ml) dark molasses or dark malt extract
    - 2 teaspoons (6 g) active dry yeast
    - 1 tablespoon (15 g) sugar or honey
    - 1 ½ teaspoons (9 g) salt
    - 2 tablespoons (30 ml) vegetable oil or melted butter
    - 1 tablespoon (10 g) caraway seeds (optional, for traditional flavor)
    - 1 tablespoon (15 g) sunflower seeds (optional, for added texture)

Instructions:

1. **Prepare the Yeast:**
    - In a small bowl, dissolve the sugar or honey in the warm water. Sprinkle the yeast over the surface and let it sit for 5-10 minutes, or until it becomes frothy and bubbly.
2. **Mix the Dough:**
    - In a large mixing bowl, combine the rye flour, whole wheat flour, all-purpose flour, and salt.
    - Make a well in the center and add the yeast mixture, molasses or dark malt extract, and vegetable oil or melted butter.
    - Stir until a rough dough forms. If using, fold in the caraway seeds and sunflower seeds.
3. **Knead the Dough:**
    - Turn the dough out onto a lightly floured surface and knead for about 8-10 minutes, or until it becomes smooth and elastic. The dough will be somewhat sticky due to the rye flour.
4. **First Rise:**
    - Place the dough in a lightly greased bowl and cover it with plastic wrap or a damp cloth.
    - Let it rise in a warm place for about 1-1.5 hours, or until it has doubled in size.
5. **Shape the Bread:**
    - Punch down the risen dough to release air. Turn it out onto a lightly floured surface.
    - Shape the dough into a loaf and place it in a greased 9x5 inch (23x13 cm) loaf pan, or shape it into a round and place it on a parchment-lined baking sheet.

6. **Second Rise:**
   - Cover the shaped loaf with plastic wrap or a damp cloth and let it rise for another 30-45 minutes, or until it has risen just above the edge of the pan or is puffy.
7. **Preheat Oven:**
   - Preheat your oven to 375°F (190°C).
8. **Prepare for Baking:**
   - If desired, sprinkle the top of the loaf with additional seeds or caraway seeds for added texture and flavor.
   - Use a sharp knife to make a few slashes on top of the loaf to allow for expansion.
9. **Bake:**
   - Bake in the preheated oven for 35-45 minutes, or until the bread is dark brown and sounds hollow when tapped on the bottom.
10. **Cool:**
    - Remove the bread from the oven and let it cool in the pan for 10 minutes before transferring it to a wire rack to cool completely.

Notes:

- **Molasses vs. Malt Extract:** Dark molasses gives a strong, sweet flavor, while malt extract adds a more complex, slightly bitter note. You can use either based on your taste preference or what you have on hand.
- **Longer Storage:** Schwarzbrot often improves with age. It keeps well and can be stored for several days, becoming more flavorful as it sits.

Enjoy your Schwarzbrot! This dense and flavorful bread pairs wonderfully with cheese, meats, or can be enjoyed simply with butter.

Gurkenbrot (Cucumber Bread)

Ingredients:

- **For the Dough:**
    - 2 ½ cups (315 g) all-purpose flour
    - 1 cup (120 g) whole wheat flour
    - 1 cup (240 g) finely grated cucumber (about 1 medium cucumber)
    - 1 cup (240 ml) warm water (110°F or 45°C)
    - 2 teaspoons (6 g) active dry yeast
    - 2 tablespoons (30 g) sugar or honey
    - 1 teaspoon (5 g) salt
    - 2 tablespoons (30 ml) olive oil or melted butter
- **For the Topping (optional):**
    - 1 tablespoon sesame seeds or poppy seeds
    - 1 tablespoon finely chopped fresh dill or chives (optional, for added flavor)

Instructions:

1. **Prepare the Cucumber:**
    - Peel the cucumber and grate it finely. Squeeze out excess moisture using a clean kitchen towel or cheesecloth. You should end up with about 1 cup of grated cucumber.
2. **Prepare the Yeast:**
    - In a small bowl, dissolve the sugar or honey in the warm water. Sprinkle the yeast over the surface and let it sit for 5-10 minutes, or until it becomes frothy and bubbly.
3. **Mix the Dough:**
    - In a large mixing bowl, combine the all-purpose flour, whole wheat flour, and salt.
    - Make a well in the center and add the yeast mixture, grated cucumber, and olive oil or melted butter.
    - Stir until a rough dough forms. The cucumber will add moisture to the dough, so it might be a bit stickier than usual.
4. **Knead the Dough:**
    - Turn the dough out onto a lightly floured surface and knead for about 8-10 minutes, or until it becomes smooth and elastic. The dough should be soft and slightly tacky due to the moisture from the cucumber.
5. **First Rise:**
    - Place the dough in a lightly greased bowl and cover it with plastic wrap or a damp cloth.
    - Let it rise in a warm place for about 1-1.5 hours, or until it has doubled in size.
6. **Shape the Bread:**
    - Punch down the risen dough to release air. Turn it out onto a lightly floured surface.
    - Shape the dough into a loaf and place it in a greased 9x5 inch (23x13 cm) loaf pan, or shape it into a round and place it on a parchment-lined baking sheet.
7. **Second Rise:**

- Cover the shaped loaf with plastic wrap or a damp cloth and let it rise for another 30-45 minutes, or until it has risen just above the edge of the pan or is puffy.

8. **Preheat Oven:**
   - Preheat your oven to 375°F (190°C).
9. **Prepare for Baking:**
   - If desired, sprinkle the top of the loaf with sesame seeds, poppy seeds, and chopped fresh dill or chives.
   - Use a sharp knife to make a few slashes on top of the loaf to allow for expansion.
10. **Bake:**
    - Bake in the preheated oven for 30-35 minutes, or until the bread is golden brown and sounds hollow when tapped on the bottom.
11. **Cool:**
    - Remove the bread from the oven and let it cool in the pan for 10 minutes before transferring it to a wire rack to cool completely.

Notes:

- **Flavor Variations:** You can add other herbs or spices to the dough, such as garlic powder or onion flakes, for extra flavor.
- **Storage:** This bread is best enjoyed fresh but can be stored at room temperature for a few days or frozen for longer storage.

Enjoy your Gurkenbrot! This refreshing bread is perfect for summer and pairs well with a variety of spreads or can be used to make light, flavorful sandwiches.

Feigenbrot (Fig Bread)

Ingredients:

- **For the Dough:**
    - 2 ½ cups (315 g) all-purpose flour
    - 1 cup (120 g) whole wheat flour
    - 1 cup (240 ml) warm water (110°F or 45°C)
    - ¼ cup (60 ml) honey or maple syrup
    - 2 teaspoons (6 g) active dry yeast
    - 1 teaspoon (5 g) salt
    - 2 tablespoons (30 ml) olive oil or melted butter
    - 1 cup (150 g) dried figs, chopped (about 10-12 figs)
    - ¼ cup (30 g) chopped nuts (optional, such as walnuts or almonds)
- **For the Glaze (optional):**
    - 2 tablespoons (30 ml) honey or maple syrup
    - 1 tablespoon (15 ml) warm water

Instructions:

1. **Prepare the Figs:**
    - Chop the dried figs into small pieces. If they are very dry, you can soak them in warm water for about 10 minutes to soften them, then drain and pat dry.
2. **Prepare the Yeast:**
    - In a small bowl, dissolve the honey or maple syrup in the warm water. Sprinkle the yeast over the surface and let it sit for 5-10 minutes, or until it becomes frothy and bubbly.
3. **Mix the Dough:**
    - In a large mixing bowl, combine the all-purpose flour, whole wheat flour, and salt.
    - Make a well in the center and add the yeast mixture, olive oil or melted butter.
    - Stir until a rough dough forms. Fold in the chopped figs and nuts (if using) until evenly distributed.
4. **Knead the Dough:**
    - Turn the dough out onto a lightly floured surface and knead for about 8-10 minutes, or until it becomes smooth and elastic. The dough may be slightly sticky due to the figs.
5. **First Rise:**
    - Place the dough in a lightly greased bowl and cover it with plastic wrap or a damp cloth.
    - Let it rise in a warm place for about 1-1.5 hours, or until it has doubled in size.
6. **Shape the Bread:**
    - Punch down the risen dough to release air. Turn it out onto a lightly floured surface.

- Shape the dough into a loaf and place it in a greased 9x5 inch (23x13 cm) loaf pan, or shape it into a round and place it on a parchment-lined baking sheet.
7. **Second Rise:**
   - Cover the shaped loaf with plastic wrap or a damp cloth and let it rise for another 30-45 minutes, or until it has risen just above the edge of the pan or is puffy.
8. **Preheat Oven:**
   - Preheat your oven to 375°F (190°C).
9. **Prepare for Baking:**
   - If desired, mix the honey or maple syrup with warm water and brush it over the top of the loaf for a shiny finish.
   - Use a sharp knife to make a few slashes on top of the loaf to allow for expansion.
10. **Bake:**
    - Bake in the preheated oven for 30-35 minutes, or until the bread is golden brown and sounds hollow when tapped on the bottom.
11. **Cool:**
    - Remove the bread from the oven and let it cool in the pan for 10 minutes before transferring it to a wire rack to cool completely.

Notes:

- **Flavor Variations:** You can add spices such as cinnamon or cardamom to the dough for extra flavor.
- **Storage:** This bread can be stored at room temperature for a few days or frozen for longer storage.

Enjoy your Feigenbrot! The combination of sweet figs and hearty whole wheat makes this bread a delicious and nutritious choice for any meal or snack.

Krustenbrot (Crusty Bread)

Ingredients:

- **For the Dough:**
    - 3 ½ cups (450 g) all-purpose flour
    - 1 ½ teaspoons (9 g) salt
    - 1 ¼ cups (300 ml) warm water (110°F or 45°C)
    - 2 teaspoons (6 g) active dry yeast
    - 1 tablespoon (15 g) sugar or honey
    - 2 tablespoons (30 ml) olive oil (optional, for a slightly softer crumb)
- **For the Steam (optional but recommended):**
    - 1 cup (240 ml) water (for creating steam in the oven)

Instructions:

1. **Prepare the Yeast:**
    - In a small bowl, dissolve the sugar or honey in the warm water. Sprinkle the yeast over the surface and let it sit for 5-10 minutes, or until it becomes frothy and bubbly.
2. **Mix the Dough:**
    - In a large mixing bowl, combine the flour and salt.
    - Make a well in the center and add the yeast mixture and olive oil (if using).
    - Stir until a rough dough forms.
3. **Knead the Dough:**
    - Turn the dough out onto a lightly floured surface and knead for about 10 minutes, or until it becomes smooth and elastic. The dough should be slightly sticky but manageable.
4. **First Rise:**
    - Place the dough in a lightly greased bowl and cover it with plastic wrap or a damp cloth.
    - Let it rise in a warm place for about 1-1.5 hours, or until it has doubled in size.
5. **Shape the Bread:**
    - Punch down the risen dough to release air. Turn it out onto a lightly floured surface.
    - Shape the dough into a round or oval loaf, or place it in a greased or parchment-lined loaf pan.
6. **Second Rise:**
    - Cover the shaped loaf with plastic wrap or a damp cloth and let it rise for another 30-45 minutes, or until it has risen just above the edge of the pan or is puffy.
7. **Preheat Oven:**
    - Preheat your oven to 450°F (230°C). If using a Dutch oven or baking stone, place it in the oven to preheat as well.

8. **Prepare for Baking:**
    - If using a Dutch oven, carefully transfer the dough to the preheated pot. If baking on a sheet, place the loaf on a parchment-lined baking sheet.
    - Use a sharp knife or bread lame to make a few slashes on top of the loaf to allow for expansion.
9. **Add Steam (optional but recommended):**
    - To create steam, place a heatproof dish of water in the bottom of the oven or carefully pour 1 cup (240 ml) of water onto the oven floor just before placing the bread in. This helps create a crispy crust.
10. **Bake:**
    - Bake in the preheated oven for 30-35 minutes, or until the bread is deep golden brown and sounds hollow when tapped on the bottom.
11. **Cool:**
    - Remove the bread from the oven and let it cool on a wire rack before slicing.

Notes:

- **Dutch Oven Baking:** If using a Dutch oven, you can cover it with a lid for the first 20 minutes of baking to create a steamy environment, then remove the lid for the last 15-20 minutes to allow the crust to crisp up.
- **Crust Variations:** For a more rustic crust, you can also sprinkle the top of the loaf with a bit of flour before baking.

Enjoy your Krustenbrot! The combination of a crispy crust and a tender, airy crumb makes this bread a perfect accompaniment to any meal or a delightful treat on its own.

Wurzelbrot (Root Bread)

Ingredients:

- **For the Dough:**
    - 3 cups (375 g) all-purpose flour
    - 1 cup (120 g) whole wheat flour
    - 1 ½ teaspoons (9 g) salt
    - 1 cup (240 ml) warm water (110°F or 45°C)
    - 2 teaspoons (6 g) active dry yeast
    - 2 tablespoons (30 ml) olive oil or melted butter
    - 1 tablespoon (15 g) sugar or honey (optional, for a touch of sweetness)
    - 1 cup (150 g) finely grated root vegetable (such as carrots, beets, or parsnips)
- **For the Topping (optional):**
    - 1 tablespoon sesame seeds or sunflower seeds
    - 1 tablespoon finely chopped fresh herbs (such as rosemary or thyme)

Instructions:

1. **Prepare the Root Vegetables:**
    - Peel and finely grate the root vegetables. Squeeze out any excess moisture using a clean kitchen towel or cheesecloth.
2. **Prepare the Yeast:**
    - In a small bowl, dissolve the sugar or honey (if using) in the warm water. Sprinkle the yeast over the surface and let it sit for 5-10 minutes, or until it becomes frothy and bubbly.
3. **Mix the Dough:**
    - In a large mixing bowl, combine the all-purpose flour, whole wheat flour, and salt.
    - Make a well in the center and add the yeast mixture, olive oil or melted butter, and the grated root vegetables.
    - Stir until a rough dough forms. The grated vegetables will add moisture, so the dough might be a bit sticky.
4. **Knead the Dough:**
    - Turn the dough out onto a lightly floured surface and knead for about 8-10 minutes, or until it becomes smooth and elastic. The dough should be soft but manageable.
5. **First Rise:**
    - Place the dough in a lightly greased bowl and cover it with plastic wrap or a damp cloth.
    - Let it rise in a warm place for about 1-1.5 hours, or until it has doubled in size.
6. **Shape the Bread:**
    - Punch down the risen dough to release air. Turn it out onto a lightly floured surface.

- Shape the dough into a round or oval loaf. You can also form it into a more traditional "root-like" shape by tapering the ends to mimic roots.
7. **Second Rise:**
   - Place the shaped loaf on a parchment-lined baking sheet or in a greased loaf pan. Cover it with plastic wrap or a damp cloth and let it rise for another 30-45 minutes, or until it has risen noticeably.
8. **Preheat Oven:**
   - Preheat your oven to 375°F (190°C).
9. **Prepare for Baking:**
   - If desired, sprinkle the top of the loaf with sesame seeds, sunflower seeds, and chopped herbs.
   - Use a sharp knife or bread lame to make a few slashes on top of the loaf to allow for expansion.
10. **Bake:**
    - Bake in the preheated oven for 35-45 minutes, or until the bread is golden brown and sounds hollow when tapped on the bottom.
11. **Cool:**
    - Remove the bread from the oven and let it cool on a wire rack before slicing.

Notes:

- **Root Variations:** Feel free to experiment with different root vegetables or combinations. Carrots add a mild sweetness, while beets give a deep color and earthy flavor.
- **Additional Flavors:** You can add spices like cumin or coriander to the dough for a unique twist.

Enjoy your Wurzelbrot! This hearty bread, with its rustic shape and subtle vegetable flavors, is perfect for hearty meals or as a standalone treat.

Apfel-Zimt-Brot (Apple Cinnamon Bread)

Ingredients:

- **For the Dough:**
    - 3 cups (375 g) all-purpose flour
    - ¼ cup (50 g) granulated sugar
    - 1 teaspoon (5 g) salt
    - 1 cup (240 ml) warm milk (110°F or 45°C)
    - 2 ¼ teaspoons (7 g) active dry yeast (1 packet)
    - ¼ cup (60 g) unsalted butter, melted
    - 1 large egg
    - 1 teaspoon vanilla extract
- **For the Apple Filling:**
    - 1 large apple, peeled, cored, and finely diced
    - ¼ cup (50 g) granulated sugar
    - 1 teaspoon ground cinnamon
- **For the Cinnamon Swirl (optional):**
    - ¼ cup (50 g) granulated sugar
    - 1 tablespoon ground cinnamon
- **For the Glaze (optional):**
    - ½ cup (60 g) powdered sugar
    - 1-2 tablespoons milk or water
    - ¼ teaspoon vanilla extract

Instructions:

1. **Prepare the Yeast:**
    - In a small bowl, warm the milk to about 110°F (45°C). Dissolve ¼ cup of granulated sugar in the warm milk and sprinkle the yeast over the surface. Let it sit for 5-10 minutes, or until it becomes frothy and bubbly.
2. **Mix the Dough:**
    - In a large mixing bowl, combine the flour and salt.
    - Make a well in the center and add the yeast mixture, melted butter, egg, and vanilla extract.
    - Stir until a rough dough forms. The dough will be slightly sticky.
3. **Knead the Dough:**
    - Turn the dough out onto a lightly floured surface and knead for about 8-10 minutes, or until it becomes smooth and elastic.
4. **Prepare the Apple Filling:**
    - In a small bowl, toss the diced apple with ¼ cup of granulated sugar and 1 teaspoon of ground cinnamon.
5. **First Rise:**

- Place the dough in a lightly greased bowl and cover it with plastic wrap or a damp cloth.
- Let it rise in a warm place for about 1-1.5 hours, or until it has doubled in size.

6. **Shape the Bread:**
   - Punch down the risen dough to release air. Turn it out onto a lightly floured surface.
   - Roll out the dough into a rectangle, about 12x18 inches (30x45 cm).
   - Evenly sprinkle the cinnamon sugar mixture (if using) over the dough.
   - Spread the apple filling evenly over the dough.
   - Starting from one edge, roll up the dough tightly into a log or cylinder shape.

7. **Second Rise:**
   - Place the rolled dough seam-side down in a greased 9x5 inch (23x13 cm) loaf pan.
   - Cover with plastic wrap or a damp cloth and let it rise for another 30-45 minutes, or until it has risen noticeably.

8. **Preheat Oven:**
   - Preheat your oven to 350°F (175°C).

9. **Bake:**
   - Bake in the preheated oven for 35-45 minutes, or until the bread is golden brown and sounds hollow when tapped on the bottom.

10. **Cool:**
    - Remove the bread from the oven and let it cool in the pan for about 10 minutes before transferring it to a wire rack to cool completely.

11. **Prepare the Glaze (optional):**
    - In a small bowl, mix the powdered sugar, vanilla extract, and just enough milk or water to achieve a smooth, drizzling consistency.
    - Drizzle the glaze over the cooled bread before serving.

Notes:

- **Apple Varieties:** Use firm apples that hold their shape well during baking, such as Granny Smith or Honeycrisp.
- **Add-Ins:** You can also add nuts or raisins to the apple filling for added texture and flavor.

Enjoy your Apfel-Zimt-Brot! This bread is wonderfully aromatic and perfect for pairing with a cup of tea or coffee. The combination of tender bread, sweet apples, and cinnamon is sure to be a hit.

Schinkenbrot (Ham Bread)

Ingredients:

- **For the Dough:**
    - 3 cups (375 g) all-purpose flour
    - 1 cup (120 g) whole wheat flour
    - 1 ½ teaspoons (9 g) salt
    - 1 cup (240 ml) warm water (110°F or 45°C)
    - 2 teaspoons (6 g) active dry yeast
    - 2 tablespoons (30 ml) olive oil
    - 1 tablespoon (15 g) sugar or honey
    - 1 cup (150 g) diced ham (cooked or cured)
    - 1 cup (100 g) shredded cheese (such as Swiss or Cheddar, optional)
- **For the Topping (optional):**
    - 1 tablespoon sesame seeds or poppy seeds
    - 1 tablespoon finely chopped fresh herbs (such as chives or parsley, optional)

Instructions:

1. **Prepare the Yeast:**
    - In a small bowl, dissolve the sugar or honey in the warm water. Sprinkle the yeast over the surface and let it sit for 5-10 minutes, or until it becomes frothy and bubbly.
2. **Mix the Dough:**
    - In a large mixing bowl, combine the all-purpose flour, whole wheat flour, and salt.
    - Make a well in the center and add the yeast mixture and olive oil.
    - Stir until a rough dough forms. Fold in the diced ham and shredded cheese (if using).
3. **Knead the Dough:**
    - Turn the dough out onto a lightly floured surface and knead for about 8-10 minutes, or until it becomes smooth and elastic. The dough will be slightly sticky due to the ham and cheese.
4. **First Rise:**
    - Place the dough in a lightly greased bowl and cover it with plastic wrap or a damp cloth.
    - Let it rise in a warm place for about 1-1.5 hours, or until it has doubled in size.
5. **Shape the Bread:**
    - Punch down the risen dough to release air. Turn it out onto a lightly floured surface.
    - Shape the dough into a loaf or divide it into smaller rolls, depending on your preference.

- Place the shaped loaf on a parchment-lined baking sheet or in a greased loaf pan.
6. **Second Rise:**
    - Cover the shaped loaf with plastic wrap or a damp cloth and let it rise for another 30-45 minutes, or until it has risen noticeably.
7. **Preheat Oven:**
    - Preheat your oven to 375°F (190°C).
8. **Prepare for Baking:**
    - If desired, sprinkle the top of the loaf with sesame seeds, poppy seeds, and chopped herbs.
    - Use a sharp knife to make a few slashes on top of the loaf to allow for expansion.
9. **Bake:**
    - Bake in the preheated oven for 30-35 minutes, or until the bread is golden brown and sounds hollow when tapped on the bottom.
10. **Cool:**
    - Remove the bread from the oven and let it cool in the pan for about 10 minutes before transferring it to a wire rack to cool completely.

Notes:

- **Ham Variations:** Use any type of ham you prefer—cooked, cured, or even leftover holiday ham. Dice it into small pieces for even distribution.
- **Cheese Options:** Feel free to experiment with different types of cheese or omit it if you prefer a simpler flavor.
- **Herbs:** Adding fresh herbs to the dough can enhance the flavor. Try chives, parsley, or dill for a fresh twist.

Enjoy your Schinkenbrot! This savory bread is perfect for making sandwiches, serving with soups, or enjoying with a simple salad. The combination of ham and cheese, with a crispy crust and soft interior, makes it a satisfying and flavorful choice.

Sonnenblumen-Dinkelbrot (Sunflower Spelt Bread)

Ingredients:

- **For the Dough:**
    - 2 ½ cups (300 g) spelt flour (whole spelt or white spelt flour)
    - 1 cup (120 g) all-purpose flour
    - 1 ½ teaspoons (9 g) salt
    - 1 ¼ cups (300 ml) warm water (110°F or 45°C)
    - 2 teaspoons (6 g) active dry yeast
    - 2 tablespoons (30 ml) honey or maple syrup
    - 2 tablespoons (30 ml) olive oil
    - ½ cup (75 g) sunflower seeds (plus extra for topping)

Instructions:

1. **Prepare the Yeast:**
    - In a small bowl, dissolve the honey or maple syrup in the warm water. Sprinkle the yeast over the surface and let it sit for 5-10 minutes, or until it becomes frothy and bubbly.
2. **Mix the Dough:**
    - In a large mixing bowl, combine the spelt flour, all-purpose flour, and salt.
    - Make a well in the center and add the yeast mixture and olive oil.
    - Stir until a rough dough forms. Fold in the sunflower seeds, ensuring they are evenly distributed throughout the dough.
3. **Knead the Dough:**
    - Turn the dough out onto a lightly floured surface and knead for about 8-10 minutes, or until it becomes smooth and elastic. The dough will be somewhat sticky due to the sunflower seeds.
4. **First Rise:**
    - Place the dough in a lightly greased bowl and cover it with plastic wrap or a damp cloth.
    - Let it rise in a warm place for about 1-1.5 hours, or until it has doubled in size.
5. **Shape the Bread:**
    - Punch down the risen dough to release air. Turn it out onto a lightly floured surface.
    - Shape the dough into a loaf or divide it into smaller rolls, depending on your preference.
    - Place the shaped loaf on a parchment-lined baking sheet or in a greased loaf pan.
6. **Second Rise:**
    - Cover the shaped loaf with plastic wrap or a damp cloth and let it rise for another 30-45 minutes, or until it has risen noticeably.

7. **Preheat Oven:**
   - Preheat your oven to 375°F (190°C).
8. **Prepare for Baking:**
   - If desired, sprinkle extra sunflower seeds on top of the loaf for added texture and visual appeal.
   - Use a sharp knife to make a few slashes on top of the loaf to allow for expansion.
9. **Bake:**
   - Bake in the preheated oven for 30-35 minutes, or until the bread is golden brown and sounds hollow when tapped on the bottom.
10. **Cool:**
    - Remove the bread from the oven and let it cool in the pan for about 10 minutes before transferring it to a wire rack to cool completely.

Notes:

- **Spelt Flour:** Whole spelt flour gives the bread a more rustic texture and richer flavor, while white spelt flour will produce a lighter texture.
- **Sunflower Seeds:** You can lightly toast the sunflower seeds before adding them to the dough for extra flavor.
- **Additional Seeds:** Feel free to mix in other seeds or nuts if desired, such as pumpkin seeds or flaxseeds.

Enjoy your Sonnenblumen-Dinkelbrot! This bread is perfect for sandwiches, toasting, or as a hearty accompaniment to soups and salads. The combination of spelt and sunflower seeds makes it both flavorful and nutritious.

Roggenbrot mit Kürbiskernen (Rye Bread with Pumpkin Seeds)

Ingredients:

- **For the Dough:**
    - 2 ½ cups (300 g) rye flour
    - 1 cup (120 g) all-purpose flour
    - 1 ½ teaspoons (9 g) salt
    - 1 cup (240 ml) warm water (110°F or 45°C)
    - 2 teaspoons (6 g) active dry yeast
    - 1 tablespoon (15 g) sugar or honey
    - 2 tablespoons (30 ml) vegetable oil or melted butter
    - ½ cup (75 g) pumpkin seeds (plus extra for topping, if desired)
- **For the Topping (optional):**
    - 2 tablespoons pumpkin seeds

Instructions:

1. **Prepare the Yeast:**
    - In a small bowl, dissolve the sugar or honey in the warm water. Sprinkle the yeast over the surface and let it sit for 5-10 minutes, or until it becomes frothy and bubbly.
2. **Mix the Dough:**
    - In a large mixing bowl, combine the rye flour, all-purpose flour, and salt.
    - Make a well in the center and add the yeast mixture and vegetable oil or melted butter.
    - Stir until a rough dough forms. Fold in the pumpkin seeds, ensuring they are evenly distributed throughout the dough.
3. **Knead the Dough:**
    - Turn the dough out onto a lightly floured surface and knead for about 8-10 minutes. Rye dough can be stickier and denser, so it may not become as smooth as wheat dough, but knead until it is well combined and elastic.
4. **First Rise:**
    - Place the dough in a lightly greased bowl and cover it with plastic wrap or a damp cloth.
    - Let it rise in a warm place for about 1-1.5 hours, or until it has doubled in size.
5. **Shape the Bread:**
    - Punch down the risen dough to release air. Turn it out onto a lightly floured surface.
    - Shape the dough into a loaf or divide it into smaller rolls, depending on your preference.
    - Place the shaped loaf on a parchment-lined baking sheet or in a greased loaf pan.

6. **Second Rise:**
   - Cover the shaped loaf with plastic wrap or a damp cloth and let it rise for another 30-45 minutes, or until it has risen noticeably.
7. **Preheat Oven:**
   - Preheat your oven to 375°F (190°C).
8. **Prepare for Baking:**
   - If desired, sprinkle extra pumpkin seeds on top of the loaf for added texture and visual appeal.
   - Use a sharp knife or bread lame to make a few slashes on top of the loaf to allow for expansion.
9. **Bake:**
   - Bake in the preheated oven for 30-40 minutes, or until the bread is deep brown and sounds hollow when tapped on the bottom.
10. **Cool:**
    - Remove the bread from the oven and let it cool in the pan for about 10 minutes before transferring it to a wire rack to cool completely.

Notes:

- **Rye Flour:** Rye flour can vary in texture. If using coarser rye flour, you might need a bit more water. If the dough feels too dry, add a small amount of water gradually.
- **Pumpkin Seeds:** Toasting the pumpkin seeds lightly before adding them to the dough can enhance their flavor.
- **Additional Seeds:** You can mix in other seeds or nuts if you like, such as sunflower seeds or flaxseeds, for additional flavor and texture.

Enjoy your Roggenbrot mit Kürbiskernen! This rye bread with pumpkin seeds is perfect for hearty sandwiches or as a side with soups and stews. The combination of the dense rye flavor and crunchy pumpkin seeds makes for a deliciously satisfying bread.

Löwenzahn-Brot (Dandelion Bread)

Ingredients:

- **For the Dough:**
    - 2 ½ cups (300 g) all-purpose flour
    - 1 cup (120 g) whole wheat flour
    - 1 ½ teaspoons (9 g) salt
    - 1 cup (240 ml) warm water (110°F or 45°C)
    - 2 teaspoons (6 g) active dry yeast
    - 2 tablespoons (30 ml) honey or maple syrup
    - ¼ cup (60 ml) olive oil or melted butter
    - 1 cup (50 g) fresh dandelion greens, finely chopped
    - ¼ cup (30 g) finely grated Parmesan or other hard cheese (optional)
- **For the Topping (optional):**
    - 1 tablespoon sesame seeds or poppy seeds
    - 1 tablespoon finely chopped fresh herbs (such as chives or parsley)

Instructions:

1. **Prepare the Dandelion Greens:**
    - Wash the dandelion greens thoroughly and remove any tough stems. Chop the leaves finely. If the greens are very bitter, you can blanch them briefly in boiling water, then chop them and squeeze out excess moisture.
2. **Prepare the Yeast:**
    - In a small bowl, dissolve the honey or maple syrup in the warm water. Sprinkle the yeast over the surface and let it sit for 5-10 minutes, or until it becomes frothy and bubbly.
3. **Mix the Dough:**
    - In a large mixing bowl, combine the all-purpose flour, whole wheat flour, and salt.
    - Make a well in the center and add the yeast mixture and olive oil or melted butter.
    - Stir until a rough dough forms. Fold in the chopped dandelion greens and grated cheese (if using), ensuring they are evenly distributed throughout the dough.
4. **Knead the Dough:**
    - Turn the dough out onto a lightly floured surface and knead for about 8-10 minutes, or until it becomes smooth and elastic. The dough will be slightly sticky due to the greens.
5. **First Rise:**
    - Place the dough in a lightly greased bowl and cover it with plastic wrap or a damp cloth.
    - Let it rise in a warm place for about 1-1.5 hours, or until it has doubled in size.
6. **Shape the Bread:**

- Punch down the risen dough to release air. Turn it out onto a lightly floured surface.
- Shape the dough into a loaf or divide it into smaller rolls, depending on your preference.
- Place the shaped loaf on a parchment-lined baking sheet or in a greased loaf pan.

7. **Second Rise:**
   - Cover the shaped loaf with plastic wrap or a damp cloth and let it rise for another 30-45 minutes, or until it has risen noticeably.
8. **Preheat Oven:**
   - Preheat your oven to 375°F (190°C).
9. **Prepare for Baking:**
   - If desired, sprinkle extra sesame seeds or poppy seeds on top of the loaf. You can also add finely chopped fresh herbs for additional flavor.
   - Use a sharp knife to make a few slashes on top of the loaf to allow for expansion.
10. **Bake:**
    - Bake in the preheated oven for 30-35 minutes, or until the bread is golden brown and sounds hollow when tapped on the bottom.
11. **Cool:**
    - Remove the bread from the oven and let it cool in the pan for about 10 minutes before transferring it to a wire rack to cool completely.

Notes:

- **Dandelion Greens:** Ensure you are using clean, pesticide-free dandelion greens. If you can't find dandelion greens, you can substitute with other leafy greens like spinach or kale.
- **Cheese:** The cheese is optional but adds a nice flavor. You can omit it or use a different type of cheese based on your preference.
- **Herbs:** Adding fresh herbs can enhance the flavor. Experiment with herbs like rosemary or thyme if you prefer.

Enjoy your Löwenzahn-Brot! This bread is a fantastic way to incorporate nutritious wild greens into your diet and makes for a flavorful, rustic loaf perfect for any meal.

Butterbrot (Butter Bread)

Ingredients:

- **For the Dough:**
    - 4 cups (500 g) all-purpose flour
    - 2 teaspoons (10 g) salt
    - 1 tablespoon (15 g) sugar
    - 1 cup (240 ml) warm milk (110°F or 45°C)
    - 2 teaspoons (6 g) active dry yeast
    - ¼ cup (60 g) unsalted butter, melted
    - 1 large egg
- **For the Topping (optional):**
    - 2 tablespoons unsalted butter, softened (for brushing on top)
    - Coarse sea salt or flaky salt (optional)

Instructions:

1. **Prepare the Yeast:**
    - In a small bowl, dissolve the sugar in the warm milk. Sprinkle the yeast over the surface and let it sit for 5-10 minutes, or until it becomes frothy and bubbly.
2. **Mix the Dough:**
    - In a large mixing bowl, combine the flour and salt.
    - Make a well in the center and add the yeast mixture, melted butter, and egg.
    - Stir until a rough dough forms. The dough will be somewhat sticky.
3. **Knead the Dough:**
    - Turn the dough out onto a lightly floured surface and knead for about 8-10 minutes, or until it becomes smooth and elastic. The dough should be slightly tacky but manageable.
4. **First Rise:**
    - Place the dough in a lightly greased bowl and cover it with plastic wrap or a damp cloth.
    - Let it rise in a warm place for about 1-1.5 hours, or until it has doubled in size.
5. **Shape the Bread:**
    - Punch down the risen dough to release air. Turn it out onto a lightly floured surface.
    - Shape the dough into a loaf by flattening it into a rectangle, then rolling it up tightly from one edge to the other.
    - Place the shaped loaf into a greased 9x5 inch (23x13 cm) loaf pan.
6. **Second Rise:**
    - Cover the loaf with plastic wrap or a damp cloth and let it rise for another 30-45 minutes, or until it has risen noticeably.
7. **Preheat Oven:**

- Preheat your oven to 375°F (190°C).
8. **Prepare for Baking:**
    - If desired, brush the top of the loaf with softened butter and sprinkle with coarse sea salt or flaky salt for extra flavor and texture.
9. **Bake:**
    - Bake in the preheated oven for 30-35 minutes, or until the bread is golden brown and sounds hollow when tapped on the bottom.
10. **Cool:**
    - Remove the bread from the oven and let it cool in the pan for about 10 minutes before transferring it to a wire rack to cool completely.

Notes:

- **Butter Application:** Brushing the loaf with butter before baking adds a nice flavor and helps to achieve a soft, golden crust.
- **Toppings:** You can also experiment with different toppings or add-ins, such as herbs, cheese, or seeds, to customize the bread to your taste.

Enjoy your Butterbrot! This bread is simple yet versatile and pairs wonderfully with a variety of spreads, from classic butter to jams, cheeses, or even savory toppings.

www.ingramcontent.com/pod-product-compliance
Lightning Source LLC
LaVergne TN
LVHW081556060526
838201LV00054B/1907